Christ in Postmodern Philosophy

# Christ in Postmodern Philosophy

## Gianni Vattimo, René Girard, and Slavoj Žižek

Frederiek Depoortere

t&t clark

**Published by T&T Clark**
*A Continuum imprint*
The Tower Building, 11 York Road, London SE1 7NX
80 Maiden Lane, Suite 704, New York, NY 10038
www.continuumbooks.com

First published 2008
Reprinted 2008

**British Library Cataloguing-in-Publication Data**
A catalogue record for this book is available from the British Library

ISBN-10:  HB: 0-567-03331-7
          PB: 0-567-03332-5
ISBN-13:  HB: 978-0-567-03331-4
          PB: 978-0-567-03332-1

Typeset by Newgen Imaging Systems Pvt Ltd, Chennai, India
Printed on acid-free paper in Great Britain by Athenaeum Press Ltd, Gatehead, Tyne and Wear

# Contents

# List of Figures and Tables

## Figures

## Tables

# Acknowledgements

In Chapter 1, subsection 3.b, a fragment from my 'Gianni Vattimo's Concept of Truth and Its Consequences for Christianity', *Theology and the Quest for Truth: Historical- and Systematic- Theological Studies* (ed. Mathijs Lamberigts, Lieven Boeve, and Terrence Merrigan; Bibliotheca Ephemeridum Theologicarum Lovaniensium, 202; Leuven, Paris, and Dudley, MA: Peeters Publishers, 2006) pp. 241–58 is used (pp. 253–55). Reproduced with kind permission by Peeters Publishers.

In chapter 2, subsection 3.a, a fragment from my 'Gianni Vattimo's Concept of Truth' is used (pp. 251–52). Reproduced with kind permission by Peeters Publishers.

Section 1 from Chapter 3 is taken from my *'Jouissance féminine?* Lacan on Bernini's "The Ecstasy of Saint Teresa" Versus Slavoj Žižek on Lars von Trier's "Breaking the Waves"', *Encountering Transcendence: Contributions to a Theology of Christian Religious Experience* (ed. Lieven Boeve, Hans Geybels, and Stijn Van den Bossche; Annua Nuntia Lovaniensia, 53; Leuven, Paris, and Dudley, MA: Peeters Publishers, 2005) pp. 21–37 (23–24 and 25–28). Reproduced with kind permission by Peeters Publishers.

Subsections 2.a, 2.b, 2.c, 2.d, 2.f, 3.a and 3.c from Chapter 3 are taken from my 'The End of God's Transcendence? On Incarnation in the Work of Slavoj Žižek', *Modern Theology* 23/4 (2007), pp. 497–523.

Material from: *On Belief*, Slavoj Žižek, Copyright © 2001 Routledge. Reproduced by permission of Taylor & Francis Books UK.

All quotations from the Bible are taken from the New Revised Standard Version.

# Abbreviations

In a number of cases, an abbreviation is used to refer to the book discussed. Full references can be found in the bibliography.

Books by Gianni Vattimo:

AC     *After Christianity*
B      *Belief*

Books by René Girard:

DDN   *Deceit, Desire, and the Novel*
DVC   'Dionysus versus the Crucified'
TH     *Things Hidden Since the Foundation of the World*
VS     *Violence and the Sacred*

Books by Friedrich Nietzsche:

AC/EH  *The Anti-Christ, Ecce Homo, Twilight of Idols and Other Writings*
KGW   *Werke: Kritische Studienausgabe*
WLN   *Writings from the Late Notebooks*

Books by Slavoj Žižek:

DSST   *Did Somebody Say Totalitarianism?*
FA      *The Fragile Absolute*
OB     *On Belief*
PD     *The Puppet and the Dwarf*
PV     *The Parallax View*
SOI    *The Sublime Object of Ideology*
TS     *The Ticklish Subject*

# Introduction

The present book offers an investigation into the Christological reflections found in the work of three contemporary thinkers, namely Gianni Vattimo, René Girard and Slavoj Žižek. It is one of the results of my doctoral research, which began in October 2003 and which intended to compare and evaluate from a theological perspective the work of a number of contemporary continental philosophers who had recently made a so-called 'turn to religion' and to monotheism in particular. The original project text mentioned the names of John D. Caputo, Richard Kearney, Gianni Vattimo, Merold Westphal and Slavoj Žižek. My first exploratory study of these philosophers suggested to me that they can be divided into two groups. The first group consists of Caputo, Kearney and Westphal. In the wake of Heidegger's announcement of the end of onto-theology and inspired by both Emmanuel Levinas and Jacques Derrida, they search for a post-metaphysical God, a God who is often indicated as *tout autre* (wholly other). Žižek, on the other hand, does not belong to this group. First, he clearly has another source of inspiration: not Heidegger, Levinas or Derrida, but Lacan and the great thinkers of German Idealism (Kant, Schelling and Hegel). Moreover, he does not aim at tracing a post-metaphysical God. His 'turn' to Christianity is a result of his concern to 'save' the achievements of modernity from fundamentalism as well as from postmodern relativism and religious obscurantism. Vattimo, finally, is a go-between. His sources (mainly Nietzsche and Heidegger) seem to indicate that he aligns with the first group. Like Caputo, Kearney and Westphal, Vattimo is also searching for the God who comes after metaphysics, but, as we shall see in due course, he explicitly rejects the wholly other God defended by them. With Žižek, furthermore, Vattimo shares the attention for the event of the incarnation and the conviction that the incarnation amounts to the end of God's transcendence. Both thinkers also defend the uniqueness of Christianity vis-à-vis natural religiosity. In this way, they seem to share at least some affinity with the views of René Girard, who has also defended the uniqueness of Christianity and claims that the latter broke away from the violent transcendence of the natural religions. In what follows, we will investigate the Christological ideas of these three contemporary thinkers, focusing on the topics of the relation between transcendence and the event of the incarnation on the one hand, and the topic of the uniqueness of Christianity on the other.

———

# Chapter 1
# Gianni Vattimo

## 1. Introducing Gianni Vattimo

In 1996, the Italian philosopher Gianni Vattimo (born in 1936) published a booklet entitled *Credere di credere* (Believing that one believes); translated into English as *Belief*.[1] In that booklet, Vattimo describes the return of religion, both in his personal life and in society. Vattimo's (re)turn to religion is closely connected to his intellectual biography. *Belief* is the final outcome of the philosophical reflection which began as the result of a political frustration. This suggests that the life of Vattimo occurs in three distinct but connected areas, namely: politics, philosophy and religion. Moreover, Vattimo's intellectual journey traces a circle. Starting from religion, the fervent Catholicism of his youth, he moved to politics and philosophy in the service of revolutionary engagement. This engagement resulted in a disillusion which was then reflected upon philosophically. This philosophical reflection eventually resulted in his return to religion. This means that Vattimo's intellectual biography contains three chapters, three periods in which each time another domain was dominant. After religion being dominant during his youth, there was successively a dominance of politics, philosophy and religion.[2] That *Belief* is closely connected to the story of Vattimo's life can also be concluded from the fact that it is written in the first-person singular while, as Vattimo mentions, he had never written in this

---

[1] Gianni Vattimo, *Credere di credere: È possibile essere cristiani nonostante la Chiesa?* (Milan: Garzanti Editore, 1996). Translated into English as: *Belief* (trans. Luca D'Isanto and David Webb; Cambridge: Polity Press, 1999) (henceforth cited as *B*).

[2] Erik Meganck, *Nihilistische caritas? Secularisatie bij Gianni Vattimo* (Tertium Datur, 15; Leuven: Uitgeverij Peeters, 2005) pp. 13–14.

3

way before in the articles and books he wrote as a professional philosopher (*B* 20).

As Vattimo tells us in *Belief* his youth was permeated by a 'fervent, even militant' Catholicism (*B* 71). He used to get up early every morning to go to mass (*B* 20) and as a teenager he became an active member and later a leader of the Catholic Action Group. He went to university in 1954, where he began to study philosophy because he wanted to combine religion and politics. In the meantime, however, Vattimo had begun to feel uncomfortable about the Church's educational system which was perceived by him as too rigid and too dogmatic. He also took offence at the Church's strong anticommunism. Like many of his young friends, Vattimo was very much in favour of a Christian socialism that would contribute to social justice. As a consequence of his political stance, he was perceived by the ecclesiastical authorities as being too radical and he was therefore asked to leave the Catholic Action. After graduating at the end of 1959 with a thesis on the concept of *poiein* (doing) in Aristotle, made under the supervision of Luigi Pareysón, he became the latter's assistant and began working on a doctorate on Heidegger. During his doctorate he stayed in Heidelberg for two years where he studied with Karl Löwith and Hans-Georg Gadamer, whose *Truth and Method* he would later translate into Italian. Vattimo finished his PhD in 1963. In 1964 he became an adjunct professor and in 1968 full professor of aesthetics at the University of Turin, where he also became chair of aesthetics and dean of the Faculty of Arts and Philosophy.[3]

In 1968, during a long period of hospitalization, Vattimo read Herbert Marcuse and other communist authors, which resulted in his 'conversion' to Maoism, a step which was taken by a lot of European intellectuals at that time. To soothe his former supervisor Pareysón, who was very worried about the direction his pupil was taking, Vattimo stressed the continuity between Pareysón himself and Marcuse as well as between Heidegger and the Marxist author Georg Lukács. Vattimo, moreover, considered Heidegger

---

[3] Santiago Zabala, 'Introduction: Gianni Vattimo and Weak Philosophy', *Weakening Philosophy: Essays in Honour of Gianni Vattimo* (ed. Santiago Zabala; Montreal & Kingston, London, and Ithaca: McGill-Queen's University Press, 2007) pp. 3–34 (5–10, 11).

to be actually more radical and revolutionary than Lukács. It is clear from this that Vattimo was never an 'orthodox' Maoist. Indeed, he always kept on reading Nietzsche and Heidegger. Based on his reading of these two major sources of inspiration, he pleaded for a broadening of the Maoist idea of revolution with an alliance between communism and the bourgeois avant-garde (and in particular with the arts and psychoanalysis). In the orthodox Marxist view, this is a strange thing to strive for, because the avant-garde is part of the superstructure and thus part of the problem which the revolution seeks to solve by intervening at the level of the infrastructure (the level of economic relationships). Yet, Vattimo wanted to avoid that the revolution would result in the dictatorship of the proletariat and therefore he defended a wider concept of revolution. This project resulted in the 1974 book *Il sogetto e la maschera: Nietzsche e il problema della liberazione* (The subject and its mask: Nietzsche and the problem of liberation), which is the most important work of Vattimo from the 1970s. It is conceived as a manifesto in which he engages both Nietzsche and Heidegger to develop a concept of cultural liberation in addition to the socio-economic liberation of Marxism. According to Vattimo, we should not only leave capitalism behind but also the Christian-bourgeois subject as analysed and criticized by both Nietzsche and Heidegger.[4]

However, this project of cultural liberation was not a success. First, the editors of *Il Manifesto*, the newspaper for which Vattimo had written *Il sogetto e la maschera* as its philosophical foundation, were not enthusiastic about the book. They were only interested in orthodox Marxism. The same was the case for the left in general. Second, and more important, during the period 1975–78 – the so-called *anni di piombo* or 'leaden years'– Maoism became increasingly violent in Turin. Radical leftists also began to target the more moderate ones, such as Vattimo, for not being radical enough and in this way betraying the revolution. In this context of violence and terror, the realization dawned on Vattimo that he had misunderstood both Nietzsche and Heidegger. It was wrong

---

[4] Meganck, *Nihilistische caritas?*, pp. 3–5. See also: Zabala, 'Introduction', pp. 10–11.

to characterize Nietzsche's overman as a revolutionary subject and to ignore Heidegger's warning that those who attempt to overcome metaphysics run the risk of lapsing into another metaphysics. The leftist activists, in their urge to eradicate the evil of the current system, would merely end up with installing an order that would be at least as violent and evil as the present one. This led Vattimo to the conclusion that we should move beyond the logic of revolution and its metaphysical violence. Or, to state it with the help of Heideggerian terminology: we should leave the logic of *Überwinding* or 'overcoming' behind and turn to a logic of *Verwinding*. This German word refers to 'turning to new purposes', 'surpassing', 'twisting', 'resigning' and 'accepting ironically'. The experience of the metaphysical and inherently violent character of revolutionary engagement brought Vattimo to a so-called 'weak interpretation' of Heidegger, which he introduced in an essay written in 1979 and in which he characterized Heidegger's ontology as 'an ontology of decline'.[5]

In that essay, metaphysics is described by Vattimo, referring to Nietzsche, as 'an attempt to master the real by force'.[6] This idea is also mentioned in the introduction to *La avventure della differenza* (The adventure of difference),[7] a collection of essays from the 1970s published in 1980 and Vattimo's first book to be translated into English. In it, he identifies metaphysics as violent: 'With its predilection for unifying, sovereign and generalizing categories, and with its cult of the *arché*, it manifests a fundamental insecurity and exaggerated self-importance from which it then reacts into over-defensiveness. All the categories of metaphysics are violent

---

[5] Meganck, *Nihilistische caritas?*, pp. 5–7. See also: Zabala, 'Introduction', pp. 12–15. The essay of Vattimo, entitled 'Verso un'ontologia del declino', has appeared in English translation as: Gianni Vattimo, 'Toward an Ontology of Decline', *Recoding Metaphysics: The New Italian Philosophy* (ed. Giovanna Borradori; Evanston, IL: Northwestern University Press, 1988) pp. 63–75.

[6] Vattimo, 'Toward an Ontology of Decline', p. 64.

[7] Gianni Vattimo, *La avventure della differenza: Che chosa significa pensare dopo Nietzsche e Heidegger* (Milan: Garzanti Editore, 1980). Translated into English as: *The Adventure of Difference: Philosophy after Nietzsche and Heidegger* (trans. C. Blamires and T. Harrison; Cambridge: Polity Press, 1993).

categories.'[8] Or, to put it differently, metaphysics is the search for a first and indubitable foundation and is therefore inherently violent. The reverse is also the case: violence is the result of metaphysical thinking, of the belief that one has access to 'objective' reality, to reality as it eternally is in itself. This was the case for the activist students that Vattimo met in his lectures in the late 1970s, some of whom were arrested and wrote letters from prison which were then read out loud during class by fellow students, letters full of metaphysics and violence.[9] On the basis of their reading of Marxist authors, these students claimed to have an insight into the true structure of reality and therefore they felt justified to act even violently against all those who hampered the full realization of this truth. Against this metaphysical violence, Vattimo states, falling back on Heidegger which he now explicitly reads through Nietzsche,[10] that we should 'leave behind Being as grounding',[11] we should no longer think of 'Being in foundational, or metaphysical, terms'. This weak interpretation of Heidegger is developed by Vattimo into a comprehensive philosophical outlook which he labels *il pensiero debole* or 'weak thought' and which is made public when, in 1983, Vattimo edits, together with Pierre Aldo Rovatti, a collection of essays under this title.[12]

---

[8] Vattimo, *The Adventure of Difference*, p. 5. See also Gianni Vattimo, 'Dialects, Difference, and Weak Thought', *Graduate Faculty Philosophy Journal* 10/1 (1984), pp. 151–64 (155–56), where Vattimo writes that:

> [T]he strong frameworks of metaphysics – *archai*, *Gründe*, primary evidences and ultimate destinies – are only forms of self-assurance for epochs in which technology and social organization had not yet rendered us capable of living in a more open horizon . . ..The ruling concepts of metaphysics turn out to be means of discipline and reassurance that are no longer necessary in the context of technology's present day dispositional activity.

[9] Zabala, 'Introduction', p. 12.
[10] Meganck, *Nihilistische caritas?*, p. 7.
[11] Vattimo, 'Toward an Ontology of Decline', p. 65.
[12] Gianni Vattimo and Pier Aldo Rovatti (eds.), *Il pensiero debole* (Milan: Feltrinelli, 1983). Vattimo's contribution to this compilation has been translated into English as 'Dialectics, Difference, Weak Thought' in the *Graduate Faculty Philosophy Journal* (see note 8 above).

In 1985, Vattimo published his main work *The End of Modernity*,[13] followed in 1986 by an edited compilation that appeared in 1988 in French translation with the explicit title *La sécularisation de la pensée* (The secularization of thought).[14] The concept of secularization has become, as we shall see in what follows, of overriding importance in the work of Vattimo and is one of the core-ideas of his thinking. In 1994, Vattimo participated in a congress dealing with philosophy of religion that took place on the island of Capri. Also Jacques Derrida and Gadamer spoke at that congress, at which Vattimo announced his return to religion.[15] This religious turn can also be concluded from the chapter on religion in his 1994 book *Beyond Interpretation*[16] and more explicitly in the aforementioned *Belief*. Vattimo has elaborated his view on Christianity in *After Christianity*, which appeared in 2002,[17] and in two dialogue books, *The Future of Religion* (together with Richard Rorty in 2004)[18] and *After the Death of God* (together

---

[13] Gianni Vattimo, *La fine della modernità: Nichilismo ed ermeneutica nella cultura postmoderna* (Milan: Garzanti Editore, 1985). Translated into English as: *The End of Modernity: Nihilism and Hermeneutics in Postmodern Culture* (trans. and intr. Jon R. Snyder; Cambridge: Polity Press, 1988).

[14] Gianni Vattimo (ed.), *Filosofia '86* (Rome: Gius, Laterza & Figli, 1986). Translated into French as: Gianni Vattimo (ed.), *La sécularisation de la pensée* (trans. Charles Alunni *et al.*; L'ordre philosophique; Paris: Editions du Seuil, 1988). Vattimo's contribution has been translated into English as: 'Metaphysics, Violence, Secularization', *Recoding Metaphysics: The New Italian Philosophy* (ed. Giovanna Borradori; Evanston, IL: Northwestern University Press, 1988) pp. 45–61.

[15] See for this: Gianni Vattimo, 'The Trace of the Trace', *Religion* (ed. Jacques Derrida, Gianni Vattimo, and Hans-Georg Gadamer; Cambridge: Polity Press, 1998) pp. 79–94.

[16] Gianni Vattimo, *Oltre l'interpretazione: Il significato dell'ermeneutica per la filosofia* (Lezioni Italiane; Rome and Bari: Laterza and Figli, 1994). Translated into English as: *Beyond Interpretation: The Meaning of Hermeneutics for Philosophy* (trans. David Webb; Cambridge: Polity Press, 1997).

[17] Gianni Vattimo, *Dopo la cristianità: Per un christianesimo non religioso* (Milan: Garzanti Editore, 2002). This book has been translated into English as: *After Christianity* (Italian Academy Lectures; New York, NY: Columbia University Press, 2002) (henceforth cited as *AC*).

[18] Santiago Zabala (ed.), *Il futuro della Religione: Solidarietà, carità, ironia* (Turin: Garzanti Libri, 2004). This book has been translated into English as: *The Future of Religion: Richard Rorty and Gianni Vattimo* (New York, NY: Columbia University Press, 2005).

with John D. Caputo in 2007).[19] In what follows, I focus on the Christological reflections which are offered by Vattimo in these recent works.

## 2. Vattimo's Heideggerian Christology: Kenosis and Caritas

Vattimo describes his rediscovery of Christianity in his 1996 book *Belief* in which he distinguishes between biographical, political and philosophical reasons for a return of religion, both in his own life and in society. First, this return is linked by Vattimo to the experience of beloved ones dying and of the discrepancy between fact and meaning, which he understands as an outcome of the process of getting old. However, these personal experiences are immediately connected by Vattimo with the *Zeitgeist*, which he describes in terms of post-revolutionary disillusionment:

> I cannot take the experience of a permanent discrepancy between existence and meaning to be an exclusively physiological fact; rather, it appears as the decisive conse-quence of a historical process in which projects, dreams of renewal, hopes even for (political) redemption, to which I had been deeply committed were shattered in a wholly contingent way (*B* 23–24).

As somebody who becomes older is confronted with limits and defeat, Vattimo suggests, contemporary society has encountered the limits of human reason and progress. Or, as Vattimo puts it, 'we believed that we could realize justice on earth, but now reckon that it is no longer possible and turn our hopes to God' (*B* 24). This seems to suggest that the return of God is bound up with the negative experiences of death, powerlessness and despair. It also seems to imply that God returns as the wholly other, who contra-dicts human rationality and ambition (*B* 24–26; see also *AC* 42

---

[19] John D. Caputo and Gianni Vattimo, *After the Death of God* (ed. Jeffrey W. Robins; Insurrections: Critical Studies in Religion, Politics, and Culture; New York, NY: Columbia University Press, 2007).

where the popularity of the idea of God as wholly other is attributed to the 'disillusionment with the revolutionary millenarianisms that have stained with bloodshed our most recent history'). As he will argue towards the end of *Belief*, however, Vattimo rejects this negative view of God. Next to a number of negative experiences, Vattimo also refers to political reasons for the return of religion, namely the fact that the impact of religious hierarchies on world politics has increased lately. In this regard, he points, for instance, to the role played by the late pope John-Paul II in the collapse of communism in Eastern Europe, which enhanced his authority with the public (*B* 26–28). Finally, there is also a philosophical reason for the return of religion, namely the retreat of modern atheism as it was found in positivism, Hegelianism and Marxism. Modern atheism was based on both the 'belief in the exclusive truth of the experimental natural sciences' and 'faith in history's progress towards the full emancipation of humanity'. Meanwhile, however, both the 'belief in objective truth' and the 'faith in the progress of Reason' have been unmasked: disenchantment has disenchanted itself, the project of demythification turned out to be the next myth. Being a philosopher, Vattimo focuses on the role philosophy played in the return of religion. In this regard, he refers to the notion of nihilism as developed by Nietzsche and Heidegger, his two main sources of inspiration. According to Vattimo, nihilism refers to 'the final consummation of the belief that Being and reality are "objective" data which thinking ought to contemplate in order to bring itself into conformity with their laws' (*B* 29) and entails the end of metaphysics, as it was announced by Heidegger (*B* 28–29).

According to Vattimo, it was his study of both Nietzsche and Heidegger who made possible the return of the Christian religion in his life. As we have seen in the previous section, ever since 1979, Vattimo has defended a so-called weak interpretation of Heidegger, which entails an interpretation of Heidegger's depiction of the history of Being as the event of the weakening or dissolution of strong structures. '[T]his means', Vattimo writes, 'that Being has a nihilistic vocation and that diminishment, withdrawal and weakening are the traits that Being assigns to itself in the epoch of the end of metaphysics and of the becoming problematic of objectivity.' Inspired by his reading of the work of

René Girard, Vattimo further explains, he came to the conclusion that Heidegger's depiction of the history of Being as the weakening of strong structures is 'nothing but the transcription of the Christian doctrine of the incarnation of the Son of God'. Moreover, Vattimo also takes a further step when he traces back his preference for the philosophies of Nietzsche and Heidegger to the Christian inheritance, which, though he thought he abandoned it, always remained influential in his life. In this way, Vattimo interprets his return to Christianity as 'the outcome of [the latter's] permanent action'. The same is the case for Heidegger's ontology of weakening as such, which is the result of the Christian message, the latter already being 'an announcement' of Heidegger's weak ontology (B 33–36). As has just been mentioned above, it was his study of Girard that inspired Vattimo to link Heidegger and the Christian doctrine of the incarnation. As indicated by Vattimo, Girard has advanced in his studies the twofold thesis that there is a close connection between violence and the sacred on the one hand, and that Christ's incarnation dismantles this violence of the sacred on the other. Vattimo is able to introduce Girard into his nihilistic philosophy, which is mainly inspired by Nietzsche and Heidegger, by identifying Girard's violent God with the God of metaphysics. Though this identification is not made by Girard himself, it is, according to Vattimo, nevertheless justified because the characteristics traditionally attributed to the God of metaphysics (such as omnipotence, absoluteness, eternity and transcendence) indicate that God is essentially violent and is, as a result, not that much different from the violent sacrality of natural religiosity (B 37–39). The core of the New Testament, in contrast, is for Vattimo the incarnation, which he interprets as 'God's abasement to the level of humanity'. In this regard, Vattimo also speaks, adopting a term from Phil. 2.7, about God's kenosis (B 39). According to Vattimo, the incarnation implies the end of an almighty, absolute, eternal God and thus the weakening of God. The God of Christianity is not the violent God of natural religiosity, and just as little the God of metaphysics who, as almighty and omniscient cause of all that is, is still in keeping with the God of the natural religions. Consequently, the end of metaphysics enables us to eventually leave that violent God behind. In this way, we can finally discover the true Christian God and realize the goal of Jesus' teaching, namely the dismantling of the violence of the sacred.

Thus, to sum up: Vattimo links an interpretation of Heidegger with one of Girard. The weakening and dissolution of strong structures – of which Heidegger spoke when he announced the end of metaphysics – is linked to the event of the incarnation – which is understood as the abasement of God and, in the line of Girard, as the dismantling of the natural sacred. The relation between the end of metaphysics and the incarnation is, more-over, double. On the one hand, it is the end of metaphysics which enables a rediscovery of the core of the biblical message (the incarnation, God's kenosis). On the other hand, the end of metaphysics is the culminating point of the movement initiated by the incarnation, namely a movement of continuing dissolu-tion, abasement, dismantling, weakening. This movement is also described by Vattimo with the help of the term 'secularization'. If the sacred is inherently violent and if the incarnation amounts to a dismantling of it, secularization – in the sense of desacraliza-tion, moving away from the sacred – is not a threat to Christianity, but, on the contrary, a realization of its essence, or, as Vattimo puts it, 'a positive effect of Jesus' teaching, and not a way of moving away from it' (*B* 41).

Although Christ came into the world to reveal the connection between the sacred and violence, and to dismantle it, the violence of the sacred has remained active within Christianity until today. It is only with the recent end of metaphysics that it is eventually dismantled. But how can we understand that Christianity itself remained under the spell of violence until now? Vattimo explains this with the help of the work of Wilhelm Dilthey, who states that, after the fall of the Roman Empire, the Christian Church was the only remaining worldly power and that therefore it was held responsible for the continuation and preservation of classical civi-lization. In this way, the Church also adopted Greek metaphysics (*B* 53; *AC* 108, 116). This metaphysics, like any metaphysics, is, as we have already seen, inherently violent, because it is the striving 'to reach and be taken up into the first principle'. In other words, metaphysics is a product of the Will to Power and arises from the human 'desire to own one's existence completely'. According to Vattimo, the violence that springs from this implies that the continuation of debate is made impossible by the authoritarian postulation of a first principle that may not be put into question (B 65[n. 18]; AC 113).

Hence Vattimo interprets the complete history of Western thought as an ongoing struggle between the objectivism of classical metaphysics and the newness introduced by Christianity, which did not immediately succeed in establishing itself completely. Vattimo thus reads the entire history of Western civilization as an exodus from the sacred into the secular, an exodus initiated by the incarnation. Consequently, according to Vattimo, secularization is not a break with Christianity. On the contrary, it is an 'application, enrichment, and specification' of the Christian origins of our Western civilization (AC 65). In this way, Vattimo considers the whole of Western civilization – characterized by scientific, economic and technical rationality – as the result of Christianity. The same applies for the Western ideas of a secular public space and the universality of reason, which are also developments of Christianity and are a continuation of it. As a result, Christians should not fear secularization. On the contrary, increasing secularization realizes the essence of Christianity.[20]

This indicates that Vattimo's return to Christianity is not an uncritical return to the doctrine of the Catholic Church. On the contrary, Vattimo accuses the official doctrine of the Church of being a rigid, metaphysical system. For, the Church is convinced of the fact that she possesses the objective truth about Being and the eternal nature of things. As a consequence, she pretends to be able to have the last word in matters of dogma and morality (B 49). In this way, the Church shares in the violence of metaphysics. Vattimo reacts against this with a plea for a drastic demythification of dogma and morality, which he describes as 'the removal of all the transcendent, incomprehensible, mysterious and even bizarre features' from the doctrine of faith. Because it is exactly 'the scandalous state' of a lot of ecclesiastical positions that makes it impossible for many contemporary human beings to join Christianity (again) and to make the choice to believe. Even if they have a sincere interest in Christianity, they are repelled by the

[20] See for this the chapters 'The West or Christianity' and 'Christianity and Cultural Conflicts in Europe' in AC 69–82 and 93–102.

rigidness of the Church's official teaching. According to Vattimo, it is by bringing to an end all 'the irrational myths, to which we are expected to adhere in the name of God's absolute transcendence, which is both metaphysical and violent', that we can attain the goal of Jesus' teaching, the dismantling of the violence of the sacred (*B* 54–55, 58, 60–62).

If one interprets, as Vattimo does, the history of Western civilization as an ever fuller realization of God's kenosis, the question should be raised of whether this process has a limit. According to Vattimo, secularization has only one limit, and that is *caritas* or charity. In *After Christianity*, he describes love as the core of the biblical revelation and as the aim, criterion and limit of a spiritual reading of Scripture. This love is 'an active commitment to diminish violence in all its forms' (*AC* 48, 51–52). In *Belief*, Vattimo speaks about 'kenosis as guided, limited and endowed with meaning, by God's love'. He elucidates this with the help of a phrase he acquires from the work of Augustine, namely '*Dilige, et quod vis fac*' ('Love, and do what you will') (*B* 64; see also *AC* 48). Furthermore, Vattimo describes the commandment of love as 'a "formal" commandment, not unlike Kant's categorical imperative, which does not command something specific once and for all, but rather applications that must be "invented" in dialogue with specific situations and in light of what holy Scriptures have revealed'. According to Vattimo, it is precisely because the commandment of love is purely formal that it cannot be secularized (*B* 66).

As we have seen above, according to Vattimo, religion mainly returns as the result of negative experiences, experiences of death, powerlessness and despair. As a result, contemporary Christianity is often of a particular character. It is described by Vattimo as 'apocalyptic', 'Dostoyevskian', 'tragic' and 'existentialist'. This kind of religiosity, which is linked by Vattimo with the names of Emmanuel Levinas and Derrida, stresses God's absolute transcendence: God is the wholly other, is incomprehensible, contradicts human reason and thwarts our plans and ambitions. This tragic or apocalyptic form of Christianity is strongly rejected by Vattimo. Against it, he writes the following:

> [I]t is merely the equally unacceptable inversion of the
> Christianity that believed that it could legitimize itself

via traditional metaphysics. Here one not only does not make any step forward in relation to the metaphysical religious nature of the past, but rather one makes a step backward. What is more authentically 'Christian', that is, farther removed from the capricious and violent deity of the natural religions: God as the supreme ground of reality, as found in Graeco-Christian metaphysics, or the wholly other of tragic religiosity inspired by existentialist thought?

If we consider the meaning of creation and redemption to be kenosis, as I believe we must in the light of the gospel, we will probably have to concede that the continuity of God and the world established by classical metaphysics is more authentically 'kenotic' than the transcendence attributed to God in naming him 'the wholly other' (B 83; see also: AC 37–39).

The defenders of the wholly other God, Vattimo adds in *After Christianity*, do not take seriously the incarnation (*AC* 43). According to Vattimo, incarnation implies that God 'is akin to finitude and nature': there is a fundamental continuity between God and world, between God and humanity. As a result, moreover, the incarnation does not invalidate non-Christian religions. On the contrary, precisely because of the incarnation, the other religions also offer ways in which God appears (*AC* 27; see also p. 98).

In a similar vein, Vattimo also rejects the view, found in Pascal and Kierkegaard, that belief asks for a leap. He attributes this view to the modern, 'strong' understanding of reason which resulted in a much too strong opposition between reason and faith (Pascal was a contemporary of arch-rationalist Descartes and Kierkegaard a contemporary of Hegel, in whom modern rationalism culminated) (*B*, 87). Vattimo further rejects the objection that he ignores God's justice and that in this way he minimizes the reality of evil and sin in the world. According to Vattimo, tragic religiosity mainly emphasizes the power of evil to bring God's saving power into sharper relief. Against this, in contrast, Vattimo stresses that the process of weakening characterizing the course of Western civilization is also affecting our understanding of sin. Since the end of metaphysics makes impossible any claim that 'good' and 'bad' are given in the nature of things, the category of sin, at least as it has traditionally been understood, as an offence against a naturally given order, turns out to be something null and void. Moreover, according to Vattimo, the view of God as a stringent and punishing judge belongs to an earlier phase of the history of civilization. In the New Testament, he claims, God's justice plays a far less important role than God's mercy. The belief in divine justice, Vattimo concludes, has to be secularized for it is not in accordance with the commandment of caritas (B 88–89).

In *After Christianity*, in which he elaborates on his view of Christianity, Vattimo adopts the theory of the three ages put forward by the twelfth-century monk Joachim of Fiore. According to the latter, history should be divided into three stages. The first stage, the one of the Father, is characterized by slavery under the law. In the human relation to God, awe is most important. The second stage belongs to the Son. In it, humans become children of God. Grace and faith play the central role in this age, in which real freedom is still not realized, however. For, as children of God, humans remain subjected to God ('filial slavery'). True freedom only appears in the age of the Spirit, in which humans become friends of God. This stage is characterized by charity (*AC* 29–30). According to Vattimo, the importance of Joachim is his view of revelation and salvation as an ongoing process, which consists in an increasing spiritualization of the meaning of Scripture. In the age of the Spirit, biblical literalism is ruled out (*AC* 26, 29, 31, 32). The letter of the scriptural texts binds us to the culture in which Scripture came into being, while through the process of leaving the literal meaning behind 'we will be able to recognize the genuine history of salvation in many aspects of the modern world and of our actuality, which instead appear to a rigorously "orthodox" mentality to be abandonment of and breaking from religion' (*AC* 47). In *After Christianity* Vattimo devotes a complete chapter to the relationship between the history of salvation and the history of interpretation. Christianity states that in Jesus salvation 'is given once and for all' (phrased differently: 'salvation is essentially "fulfilled" in the incarnation, death, and resurrection of Jesus'). Jesus is the final interpretation of the Law and the Prophets. His resurrection, however, is not the end of all interpretation. For, the message of salvation needs 'interpretations that receive it, actualize it, and enrich it'. Seemingly, salvation thus asks for 'a further fulfilment'. According to Vattimo, this fulfilment takes place through the hermeneutical labour of the faithful, who are assisted in this task by the Holy Spirit. As a consequence, interpretation is not merely a means to understand revelation, but on the contrary a constitutive part of it. The interpretation of Scripture is essential for the history of salvation (*AC* 59–60). Vattimo puts this as follows:

> The history of salvation that continues in the age of the Spirit . . . is not simply driven by the biological fact of the presence of ever new human generations that must be evangelized. . . . This history has a meaning and a direction, and the interpretation of Scripture that takes place in it is its constitutive dimension. It is not only a tale of errors, or conversely of close or literal understanding of meaning given once and for all in Scripture . . . . *The history of salvation continues as the history of interpretation* in the strong sense in which Jesus himself was the living, incarnate interpretation of Scripture (*AC* 60–61; emphasis added).

This relationship between the history of salvation and history of interpretation enables Vattimo to interpret hermeneutics as a product of Christianity. The Jesus-event is itself already essentially hermeneutical; Jesus is the living interpretation of the Law and the Prophets. Moreover, the Christian view on revelation and salvation – like it is sketched above – results in the idea of *productive interpretation*. This implies that interpretation 'is not only an attempt to grasp the original meaning of the text (for example, the authorial intention) and to reproduce it as literally as possible but also to add something essential to the text'. Furthermore, the idea of productive interpretation is itself a new step in the history of salvation, which – as is indicated – continues as the history of interpretation (*AC* 62–63).

## 3. Evaluation

Vattimo's proposal for a postmodern Christianity raises many questions. In what follows I shall first list a number of such questions before examining whether Vattimo is not merely repeating 'God is dead'-theology.

## a. Questions for Vattimo

1. First, we can have doubts about the way Vattimo reads Nietzsche and Heidegger. In this regard, it should be noted that, while Vattimo is appealing to Nietzsche and Heidegger to defend nihilism, these authors were actually stating that we have to move beyond nihilism.[21] It is also doubtful whether it is correct to engage Nietzsche in order to defend a nihilistic pluralism, as Vattimo does. According to Theo de Wit, Nietzsche rejects such a pluralism and the great challenge faced by the *Übermensch* is precisely to overcome it.[22]

2. A second question is whether Vattimo is justified in identifying metaphysics and violence. Is it not possible that there is metaphysics without violence? Why would transcendence always have to be violent *by definition*? What about non-metaphysical violence, violence that cannot be traced back to metaphysical presuppositions?[23] With regard to the problematic of violence, we should, as Peter Jonkers does, also raise the question of whether Vattimo's weak thought is able to reduce violence. According to Jonkers, this is not the case. (a) First, Vattimo's thought remains dualistic: '[I]t is stuck in an oppositional way of thinking, in a dualism of strong versus weak, violent versus non-violent, established objectivity versus nihilistic openness'. Jonkers adds that such dualisms are precisely characteristic of the metaphysical tradition, which Vattimo wants to contend with and, moreover, this dualistic thought is violent because it is an attempt to schematize plural reality in

---

[21] Cf. Meganck, *Nihilistische caritas?*, pp. 168, 171, 186–87. See also: Theo W.A. de Wit, 'The Return to Religion: Vattimo's Reconciliation of Christian Faith and PostModern Philosophy', *Bijdragen* 61/4 (2000), pp. 390–411 (399). See also: W. Müller-Lauter, 'Nietzsche und Heidegger als nihilistische Denker: Zu Gianni Vattimos "postmodernistischer" Deutung', *Nietzsche-Studien* 27 (1998), pp. 52–81.

[22] de Wit, 'The Return to Religion', pp. 400–02.

[23] Cf. Meganck, *Nihilistische caritas?*, p. 169 and p. 190.

clear-cut categories. (b) Second, Vattimo's weak thought is not able to cancel or even reduce 'the real violence of discipline and normalisation'. It merely reverses the modern subject–object scheme, leaving that scheme intact, while, in Jonkers's view, the subject-object division is as such a source of violence. (c) Third, Vattimo does not acknowledge the violence of 'subjectivist reason'. Jonkers describes this violence as 'the ruthless will of the contingent, historical subject to dissolve all substantiality, anything which gives content to life, whatever is sufficiently worthwhile for people to devote their lives to, by considering them as constructions of the finite and local subject'. Why would this kind of universalistic tendency be less violent than the universalistic pretensions of objective reason? And why, furthermore, would universality and objectivity be as such violent?[24]

3.  Third, the question should be raised whether Vattimo's weak thought is truly free from metaphysics. (a) First, we can suspect that he deals with the history of philosophy in a metaphysical manner by unifying and totalizing it under the label of 'metaphysics'. Is it not a form of violence to reduce thinkers as divergent as Plato, Aristotle, Augustine, Aquinas, Kant and Hegel to one category, namely the one of metaphysical thinkers?[25] (b) There is also another problem that should be mentioned here. Though Vattimo designates his view of the history of Being as the event of weakening as 'just' an interpretation, he nevertheless uses it as a criterion to judge and condemn alternative views, such as metaphysical nostalgia, tragic religiosity and de-secularization. But if he does not claim to offer a true, objective description of reality, how can such a condemnation then ever be justified? How can he know that metaphysics will never come back again? Or even: that metaphysics *should* never come back again?[26] (c) Also the very idea of *Verwindung* is problematic. What does it, for instance, mean to weaken Plato? What is left of the Platonic Forms after they

[24] Peter Jonkers, 'In the World, but not of the World: The Prospects of Christianity in the Modern World', *Bijdragen* 61/4 (2000), pp. 370–89 (382–83).
[25] Cf. Meganck, *Nihilistische caritas?*, pp. 168–69.
[26] Cf. Meganck, *Nihilistische caritas?*, pp. 191, 193.

have been *verwunden*? And is it not nonsense to speak about a weakened Platonic Form?[27]

4. Fourth, there is also the problematic role of caritas. As we have seen, caritas functions as a kind of categorical imperative, which directs and limits the process of secularization. It thus seems that caritas turns out to be something absolute, something transcendent, namely a principle that is valid always and everywhere and, as a consequence, is not bound to time or place. In Vattimo's weak thought, however, there is no place for such an absolute principle, because 'weak thinking dissolves every fixed meaning of humanity and the world into a thoroughly contingent, historical and local occurrence. In such a world, everything is hypothetical, i.e. subject to circumstance, place and time.' Jonkers thus concludes as follows:

> Consequently, the limiting of secularization by the commandment of love is nothing but *an arbitrary decision on the part of Vattimo as an individual*. Once thinking begins to unmask every representation of the sacral, as well as the sacral itself, . . . it cannot stop short at the commandment of love as something sacrosanct anymore. If one wants to do this nevertheless, then such a decision appears from the perspective of radical nihilism as *an expression of violent arbitrariness*.[28]

5. A fifth remark concerns Vattimo's reading of Girard. Though the latter is honoured by Vattimo as the author who enabled him to link his weak thought and Christianity, the question should be raised to what extent Vattimo has really taken Girard seriously. We return to this question in the next chapter in which we shall deal with Girard.

6. A sixth remark concerns Vattimo's view of the non-Christian world religions. With regard to Judaism, it should be noted that Vattimo explicitly designates the tragic religiosity which he opposes as 'Judaic' (*B* 84) and he characterizes it as a return to the God of the Old Testament (*B* 83; *AC* 37). In this way,

[27] Cf. Meganck, *Nihilistische caritas?*, pp. 169–70, 171.
[28] Jonkers, 'In. the world, but not of the world,' p. 386.

Vattimo is magnifying the discontinuity between the Old and the New Testament. The God of the Old Testament is then characterized by him as transcendent, wholly other, Father, severe, violent while the key terms of the New Testament are incarnation, kenosis, secularization, Spirit and love. Though Vattimo stresses that he has no anti-Semitic intentions (*B* 84; *AC* 37), this opposition between a tragic religiosity which is designated as Judaic and Vattimo's own form of Christianity nevertheless seems to imply that, in Vattimo's view, Judaism cannot but be superseded. In this way, Vattimo tends towards anti-Judaism, or at least to supercessionism, i.e. the view that Christianity fulfils Judaism, leaving no room for a non-Christian Judaism. Vattimo's relation towards Islam is equally difficult. For instance, in *After Christianity*, he sides with the defenders of the *laïcité* opposing the wearing of the chador in public schools or by officials. In Vattimo's view, the chador amounts to nothing less than a 'profession of fundamentalism'. A crucifix, in contrast, is only a reminder of the religious origin of Western secularity and should therefore not be a reason for offence (*AC* 101–02). This suggests that Vattimo is opposing Islam because it is not kenotic and does not accept the consequences of the incarnation. With regard to the non-monotheistic religions, Vattimo states that the incarnation entails that truth may be found in them as well (*AC* 100), but it is difficult to see how this fits in with the rest of his Christological reflections.

7.  A seventh remark concerns the way Vattimo deals with the content of the Christian tradition. It is clear that his version of Christianity is a very reduced one. (a) References to Scripture are limited to a phrase from Jn 15.15 and Phil. 2.7, which are read completely isolated from any context. (The same applies for the phrase on love which he picks from the work of Augustine.) (b) Vattimo's version of kenosis is a very poor one. He only reads half of the Christological hymn found in Philippians 2 and simply skips the part in which the *exaltation* of Christ is mentioned. (c) The incarnation indeed plays a role in his philosophy, but without the cross and without the resurrection. (d) His understanding of the Trinity is quite heterodox: he follows the Trinitarian epochalism of the

twelfth-century monk Joachim of Fiore, which entails that Father, Son and Spirit are not Persons, but modes in which God appears in subsequent ages (modalism). (e) Vattimo also depersonalizes God: God disappears, dissolves in the world, becomes the message about the caritas. (f) Vattimo pays no attention to the life of the historical Jesus and (g) completely ignores the eschatological and even apocalyptic character of the latter's proclamation (no Judgment, no place for God's justice). Finally, there is in Vattimo's weak thought no room, (h) neither for the traditional Christian hope for resurrection and eternal life with God, (i) nor for religious practices such as prayer.[29] All this suggests that the Christianity which has returned in Vattimo's life is a very weak, merely philosophical, version of Christianity. This also makes clear that in the third period of Vattimo's life, of which I have said at the beginning of this chapter that it was dominated by religion, it is actually philosophy which remains dominant. In that third period, weak thought indeed becomes religious, it receives the Christian tradition, but that tradition can only enter when it subjects itself to the conditions put forward by weak thought. In Vattimo's thought, there is no moment at which the tradition casts doubts on weak thought. There is no interchange between philosophy and the Christian tradition. The religious tradition is merely adapted, dissolved even. This seems to indicate that Vattimo's weak thought is not really hospitable to Christianity but rather reduces it to itself. Which is, one has to admit, quite a violent procedure.

## b. Vattimo's Christology, a 'God Is Dead'-Theology in Disguise

As we have seen, according to Vattimo, the incarnation amounts to the end of God's transcendence (the death of the God of beyond). This idea is not new. It had already been defended by Thomas J.J.

---

[29] A number of these criticisms have also been pointed out by Anthony C. Sciglitano, jr. in his 'Contesting the World and the Divine: Balthasar's Trititinitarian "Response" to Gianni Vattimo's Secular Christianity', *Modern Theology* 23/4 (2007), pp. 525–59. We return to this paper in Chapter 3, section 3.b.

Altizer in his *The Gospel of Christian Atheism*.[30] Altizer was one of
the most colourful proponents of a short-lived theological movement which boomed some forty years ago, in the mid-1960s of
the previous century: the so-called 'God is dead'-theology. It was
with the 'God is dead'-theology that late-modern theology reached
a climax (or, depending on one's perspective, a rock bottom). Late-
modern theology had come into being when a number of Christian
theologians wanted to value the achievements of modernity positively. As Lieven Boeve indicates in *Interrupting Tradition*, in order
to do this, these theologians adopted the modern critique of religion and legitimated modernity as the outcome of Christianity,
by stating that the secularizing tendencies of modernity were
already part of the Biblical message.[31] This strategy was the most
radically implemented by Altizer and his colleague 'God is dead' -
theologians.

Starting from the opposition between Christianity and 'the religions', an opposition derived from Karl Barth, Altizer's *The Gospel
of Christian Atheism* raises the question of the uniqueness of Christianity. The religions, Altizer claims, all share to some degree in an
attitude of contempt for the world. Religion is the human attempt
to escape from the 'here and now' through a flight in a 'beyond' and
is therefore 'a backward movement of return to an original sacred'.
Christianity, in contrast, despite the fact that it has been for the
largest part of its history also, or even mainly, religious, nevertheless
contains, according to Altizer, a non-religious core.[32] This non-
religious core is the event of the incarnation, which is 'an actual

---

[30] Thomas J.J. Altizer, *The Gospel of Christian Atheism* (Philadelphia, PA: The
Westminster Press, 1966).
[31] Lieven Boeve, *Interrupting Tradition: An Essay on Christian Faith in a Postmodern
Context* (trans. Brian Doyle; Louvain Theological and Pastoral Monographs,
30; Leuven and Dudley, MA: Peeters Press and W.B. Eerdmans, 2003)
pp. 45–46.
[32] See: Altizer, *The Gospel of Christian Atheism*, pp. 31–40 (quotation from p. 39).
Altizer enumerates the following religious elements of historical Christianity:

A nostalgia for a lost paradise, a quest for an original innocence, a cultic
re-presentation or recollection of a sacred history of the past, a conception of faith as contemporaneity with an ancient or long distant epiphany
of Christ, a belief in a primordial God whose very sacrality annuls or
negates the existence of the profane, and a longing for an eschatological
End that will be a repetition of the primordial Beginning (pp. 39–40).

movement of Spirit's decisively and truly becoming flesh'.[33] Historical Christianity, however, has not yet understood the incarnation
radically enough, because its understanding of it remained bound to
a religious frame. In this way, the radicality of the incarnation was
neutralized: we do not take the incarnation seriously as long as we
continue to combine the doctrine of the incarnation with a belief
in 'a transcendent, a sovereign, and an impassive God'. '[T]he Word
cannot be . . . fully man', Altizer claims, 'if, . . . it [also] continues to
exist in an eternal form'. For, in that case 'it is unable to move into
the present and the full reality of history'. As a result, Christians only
take the incarnation seriously when they free themselves, not only
of the religious contamination of Christianity, but also of its infec-
tion by the 'Greek metaphysical idea of God as an eternal and
unmoving Being'. In *The Gospel of Christian Atheism*, this is put as
follows:

> Thus the radical Christian reverses the orthodox confes-
> sion, affirming that "God is Jesus" . . ., rather than "Jesus
> is God". Before the Incarnation can be understood as a
> decisive and real event, it must be known as effecting a
> real change or movement in God himself: God becomes
> incarnate in the Word, and he becomes fully incarnate,
> thereby ceasing to exist or to be present in his primordial
> form. To say that "God is Jesus" is to say that God has
> become the Incarnate Word, he has abandoned or negated
> his transcendent form; or rather, he remains present and
> real in his original form only where faith itself refuses to
> become incarnate.[34]

Thus, to sum up: after the incarnation, there is no longer a
transcendent God. God has fully given Godself: the Spirit has
become flesh completely and there is no Spirit left behind anymore. The incarnation is a kenotic movement, resulting in the
total abandonment of God's 'original and primordial form', of
God's 'original purity and power'.[35] The incarnation, moreover, is,

---

[33] Altizer, *The Gospel of Christian Atheism*, p. 41.

[34] Altizer, *The Gospel of Christian Atheism*, pp. 41–44.

[35] Altizer, *The Gospel of Christian Atheism*, p. 53.

according to Altizer, not 'a final once-and-for all event of the past', but 'an active and forward-moving process, a process that even now is making all things new'.[36] The process initiated by the incarnation is one of a transition from the sacred into the profane. 'Christianity', Altizer states, 'proclaims the death of the sacred.'[37] He therefore concludes the first chapter of his *The Gospel of Christian Atheism* as follows:

> In the Crucifixion the Word has finally died to its original form, losing its transcendent glory and its primordial holiness, while fully becoming flesh. Only in the Crucifixion, in the death of the Word on the Cross, does the Word actually and wholly become flesh. Finally, the Incarnation is only truly and actually real if it effects the death of the original sacred, the death of God himself.[38]

In *After Christianity*, Vattimo mentions the name of Altizer, but he opposes him and other 'God is dead'-theologians (including Bonhoeffer among them) because they have not offered a 'positive affirmation of divinity based on the idea of the incarnation' (*AC* 37). Yet, when we compare Altizer's and Vattimo's interpretation of the incarnation, we find a number of remarkable similarities: (1) First, both authors share the Barthian idea that there is a clear distinction between Christianity on the one side and natural religiosity on the other. Natural religiosity chains humankind to the sacred, while a well-understood (i.e., a secularized) Christianity enables human beings to break these chains of the natural sacred. (2) Second, for both Vattimo and Altizer, the core of Christianity is the event of the incarnation. Both authors interpret the incarnation as the end of God's transcendence, as the death of the 'God of beyond'. They both use the term 'kenosis' and consider the incarnation as the start of a process of desacralization and secularization. (3) Third, according to both Vattimo and Altizer, the true meaning of the incarnation has only recently been exposed. For, until recently, that meaning had been wrapped up in,

[36] Altizer, *The Gospel of Christian Atheism*, p. 41.
[37] Altizer, *The Gospel of Christian Atheism*, p. 51.
[38] Altizer, *The Gospel of Christian Atheism*, p. 54.

and therefore neutralized by, a religious frame and metaphysical ideas. In this way, both authors seem to imply that Greek metaphysics was still an expression of natural religiosity and, as such, contaminated by the sacred. (4) Fourth, Vattimo and Altizer share the presupposition that transcendence cannot but be violent and oppressive. For both, the end of transcendence is therefore welcomed as a liberation.[39] (5) Finally, for both authors, the death of God is not a metaphor for a change in human experience, but part of the life of the Absolute itself. Vattimo interprets, as we have seen above, the history of Being, in the line of Heidegger, as a continuing process of dissolution, abasement, dismantling, weakening, secularization, and the incarnation as the announcement and cause of this process. In a similar vein, Altizer stresses that it was God who took the initiative to empty himself (cf. Phil. 2.7). In this regard, he speaks, in Hegelian style, about God's self-negation: 'God has negated *himself* in becoming flesh, his Word is now the opposite or the intrinsic otherness of his primordial Being, and God *himself* has ceased to exist in his original mode as transcendent or disincarnate Spirit.'[40]

Interpreting secularization as the outcome of Christianity was not limited to the so-called 'God is dead'-theologians, but was a strategy generally adopted by late-modern theologians. For instance, as far back as the 1960s, both Arend Theodoor van Leeuwen and Edward Schillebeeckx, interpreted secularization as a consequence of the Biblical message and stated that secularization already commences in the book of Genesis.[41] Thus, although Vattimo is arguing on the basis of Nietzsche and Heidegger, he is actually repeating a strategy of many late-modern theologians. This raises the question of whether Vattimo is in this way not offering old

[39] See, for instance: Altizer, *The Gospel of Christian Atheism*, p. 71: '[The death of God] has liberated humanity from the oppressive presence of the primordial Being.'

[40] See: Altizer, *The Gospel of Christian Atheism*, p. 69 (emphases added).

[41] See e.g. Arend Theodoor van Leeuwen, *Christianity in World History: The Meeting of the Faiths of East and West* (trans. Hubert H. Hoskins; forew. Hendrik Kraelmer; London: Edingburgh House Press, 1964) and Edward Schillebeeckx, 'Secularization and Christian Belief in God', *God the Future of Man* (trans. N.D. Smith; Theological Soundings, 5,1; London and Sydney: Sheed and Ward, 1969) pp. 51–90.

wine in new bottles. Is he not using a strategy that has already been seriously discredited by the criticism of many contemporary theologians who have rejected the so-called 'modern correlation method', by which their late-modern colleagues had attempted to 'correlate' the Christian tradition and the secular context? Or does Vattimo's analysis of the postmodern situation, on the contrary, demonstrate that we should rehabilitate this often discredited method?

The modern correlation method was, as already mentioned, used by many late-modern theologians to relate and reconcile Christianity and secular, modern culture. The late-modern theologians using this method stated, for instance, that it is by participating in the modern attempts to create a just and good society that Christians are doing their part in realizing God's dream with humanity. In *God Interrupts History*, Boeve enumerates four presuppositions of the modern correlation method. (a) The correlation method is based on an analysis of the contemporary situation in terms of secularization. (b) Modern theologians using this method have great faith in the modern project of progress and emancipation. (c) They are convinced that there is no contradiction between a well-understood modernity and the essence of Christianity. (d) Moreover, it is important to keep in mind the context in which the correlation method came into being: it has been developed in a society which was still largely Christian or which was at least still familiar with the Christian tradition.[42] These four presuppositions can also be found in the thought of Vattimo. First, he offers an analysis in terms of secularization. Second, as did the enlightened thinkers, he wants to defend freedom and emancipation against the violence of old metaphysical beliefs, myths and ideologies. In this regard, it is important that Vattimo is not 'preaching a pure and simple return to myth and ideology without setting up any critical principle' (*AC* 20). Third, he understands modernization, interpreted in terms of secularization and as the weakening of strong structures, as the outcome and realization of Christianity. And fourth, as he tells in both *Belief*

---

[42] Lieven Boeve, *God Interrupts History: Theology in Times of Upheaval* (London and New York, NY: Continuum, 2007) pp. 44–45.

and *After Christianity*, he was raised as a Catholic in a time in which Italian society was still dominantly Christian (*B* 20; *AC* 2–3). We may thus suppose that he has a basic familiarity with the Christian tradition.

In the past decade, however, the modern correlation method has been severely criticized. As Boeve makes clear, its presuppositions have been put into question. (a) First, it is no longer certain whether an analysis in terms of secularization is still the most appropriate way to understand the contemporary situation of religion. Many sociologists of religion have questioned the classic paradigm of secularization and have stated that religion has changed rather than disappeared. As Boeve mentions, there is no longer a monolithic secular culture challenging Christianity. Christians are now confronted with a wide plurality of religions and ideologies. (b) Second, the modern project of progress and emancipation, in which the modern theologians had such a great faith, has been put into question. Postmodern philosophers have criticized the modern master-narratives as hegemonic, violent and totalitarian. (c) Third, the compatibility of Christianity and modernity has been put into question. Anti-modern theologians state that their modern colleagues are merely conforming Christianity to a sinful and arrogant modernity; while those inspired by postmodern sensibilities evaluate the modern correlation method as an unjustified theological recuperation, attempting to reincorporate into Christianity things that are not or no longer Christian. (d) Moreover, we should take into account that the still largely Christian society in which the correlation method had been developed has meanwhile disappeared. As a result, interpreting human experiences, such as the desire for fulfilment and liberation, immediately as Christian experiences is probably no longer accepted by those having these experiences;[43] which amounts to saying that the correlation method has simply lost its starting point.

Inspired by his study of postmodern thinkers, Boeve no longer attempts to formulate the Christian narrative in terms of the generally-human and a general religiosity. Starting from an

---

[43] Boeve, *God Interrupts History*, pp. 45–46.

analysis of the contemporary situation in terms of pluralization, Boeve stresses *the specificity of the Christian narrative*. The most important problem of the modern correlation method is indeed that it ultimately led to a relativization of the narrative particularity of Christianity. To demonstrate this, we can refer to another aspect of modern theology, namely the way it often dealt with the Bible. When, for instance, confronted with the fact that the natural sciences seem to refute many details of the Gospel narratives, modern theologians often reacted by making a distinction between the message of the Gospel and its narrative expression. In this regard we can refer to Rudolf Bultmann's project of demythologization. Bultmann stated that the Biblical world view is thoroughly mythological and can, as such, no longer be adopted by us, modern humans living in an age of science. It is, however, according to Bultmann, possible to extract a timeless and eternal message from the Gospels. Unfortunately, when Bultmann formulated this unchanging basic message, it proved to be by and large his very particular Heideggerian, existentialist philosophy. This seems to be the deadlock of any attempt to deduce a timeless basic message from the Gospel narratives: it always tends to end up injecting a particular contemporary philosophy into the Gospel. In this way, the Gospel narratives become only a 'narrative doubling' of that philosophy and, as a result, the question very quickly arises as to why we should hold on to these often difficult and obscure narratives, when we can read the same philosophy with more clarity in the philosophy text books.

A similar kind of question should be asked to Vattimo. As we have pointed out, Vattimo pleads for a 'demythification' of dogma and morality, which he describes as 'the removal of all the transcendent, incomprehensible, mysterious and even bizarre features' from the doctrine of faith. The question certainly should be asked whether in this way Vattimo is not reducing Christianity to some vague doctrine, in which, in the end, the Biblical God completely disappears from view and is replaced by an abstract and formal principle, that of caritas. Would that not be the logical outcome of his undertaking? Thus, to conclude: Vattimo does not take the God of the Bible seriously. Indeed, for Vattimo such a God is much too metaphysical and he is much too modern to return to such a God. He cannot and does not want to rehabilitate the old beliefs because they have been, and still are, a source of intolerance and violence. So, when dealing with the Bible, he is repeating the strategy of many modern theologians. As they have done before him, he tries to deduce a basic message from the Biblical text and finds that core in the ideas of kenosis and caritas. In this way, however, Vattimo is turning the Biblical story on God's kenosis in Christ into a narrative double of his own nihilistic philosophy, reducing the narrative particularity of the Bible to a vague and soft message on friendliness.

Boeve is correct in questioning such reductions and in stressing that we do not have an access to the generally human *in abstracto*, but only possess particular fillings-in of it and that we should, therefore, take these particular fillings-in seriously. It should be kept in mind, however, that this is neither a plea for postmodern relativism nor for narrative closure or fundamentalism. (a) The claim that truth can only be found *in* the particular should not be confused with the one that truth is merely particular, never transcends a particular narrative frame or does not get beyond its being bound to a certain time and place. Attention for the particular character of our truth claims does not imply that we are denying the fact that these truths do indeed lay claim to being of universal validity. (b) Moreover, the particular character of truth claims does not mean that all such claims are equally valid and that we can therefore as well re-establish our own narrative as a master-narrative, rejecting every rational account of our own particular beliefs. In each case, the particular character of our truth claims does not mean that we can abandon *the rational explanation of our own particular position*. It is not because all truth claims arise from a particular context and that we have no God's eye point of view, no non-involved perspective to judge these competing claims, that dialogue between different positions has become impossible or that people have to remain locked up in their own narrative, in their own 'separate universe of discourse'. This does not take away, however, that it is highly unlikely that this dialogue will ever result in a kind of Hegelian *Aufhebung* of differences in a higher unity, in a generally human consensus beyond the many particular positions participating in the dialogue. Or to put it differently, we can only speak a particular language. Even if we would attempt to construct a kind of religious Esperanto in order to transcend the differences between particular religions, we are actually only creating one more particular language.

All this does not take away, however, that the question of the relation between Christianity and secularization is still unanswered. As we have seen, both the philosopher Vattimo and the theologian Altizer confirm this relation and they even claim that secularization is the essence of Christianity. Both authors identify, as we have outlined, the incarnation as the starting point of the process of secularization. Their respective views, however, are problematic; and this for two reasons: (1) First, they do not leave much room for a future for Christianity after secularization. On the basis of their work, the conclusion seems inevitable that Christianity did indeed play an irreplaceable role in the dismantling of the sacred, but that, with the arrival of secular civilization, the role of Christianity is played out. Thus, in this regard, the destiny of Christianity seems to be fulfilled when it has abolished itself. If Vattimo and Altizer are correct, Christianity is indeed 'the religion of the exit of religion' (Marcel Gauchet). In this way, however, the christologies of Vattimo and Altizer amount to a legitimization of secularization, seemingly without any reservation. (2) Moreover, both Vattimo and Altizer remain too philosophical, too spiritual, too idealistic. Their views are not grounded in an anthropology which also takes into account the human being as a physical and material creature. Their account of secularization is also not linked to a view on what the human being is and on what makes the human being human. This becomes clear from the way they speak about 'the sacred', which remains a vague category for them. But because of this, also their claim that the incarnation marks the end of the natural sacred lacks concreteness. The fact that Vattimo and Altizer, in their attempt to evaluate secularization positively from a Christian perspective, end up with simply offering a Christian legitimization of the abandonment of Christianity, raises the question of whether such a positive evaluation of secularization is possible at all.

This does not take away, however, that Vattimo and Altizer raise legitimate questions concerning the relation of Christianity to the sacred on the one side and with the process of secularization on the other. They ask, moreover, for the universal importance of

Christianity, for its generally human truth. These questions concern 'the uniqueness of Christianity', to put it with the title of the first chapter of Altizer's *The Gospel of Christian Atheism*, and are still relevant in our so-called post-secular situation. We can point out three main reasons for this enduring relevance.

1.  First, the fact that an analysis in terms of 'pluralization' seems to offer a more adequate description of the contemporary situation of religion than one in terms of 'secularization' does not mean that we no longer live in a context characterized by the effects of a process of secularization. Modernity may indeed not have resulted in a complete disappearance of religion, that does not imply that desacralization, the end of transcendence, the death of God and the loss of a sacramental-participative world view are no longer part of our daily experience in the West. It should indeed be kept in mind that, at least in the West, many forms of contemporary religiosity, tend to stress inner-worldliness and the immanence of the divine. In this regard, they are rather a confirmation of secularization than a refutation of it. Moreover, we should also keep in mind that many contemporaries do not seem to be interested in religion at all: seemingly, practical atheism and religious indifference are widespread.

2.  Second, precisely the contemporary religious plurality should confront us again with the question of the uniqueness of Christianity. Indeed, when there is a multiplicity of positions on the religious field, that question becomes inevitable; unless we want to make of Christianity merely one religion among many possibilities to which we adhere by habit, tradition, or taste. If we want to avoid this, we have to justify why we remain a Christian and this has to be done in terms which can be understood by our fellow human beings, irrespective of whether they share our Christian horizon or not. This makes clear, moreover, that the contemporary awareness of the particularity of the Christian narrative does not mean that Christians must give up apologetics, in the sense of the rational explanation of the Christian narrative in a way which is also understandable for those who are not involved in the Christian tradition. Theology should still be *fides quaerens intellectum*,

faith seeking understanding, an understanding which can only be reached by entering into dialogue with the contemporary context.

3. Third, the possibility of a naturalistic explanation of religious phenomena (including Christianity) which is offered by natural science entails that answering the question of Christian uniqueness should take the form of a search for the irreducible otherness of Christianity vis-à-vis generally human, natural religiosity; a search which has to take its start from within the natural condition of humankind, because, in the light of the naturalistic critique of Christianity, we can no longer take the supernatural origin of Christianity for granted. This confronts us with two questions. *On the one side*, we have to ask what the natural sacred is and where it comes from. *On the other side*, we have to raise the question of how Christianity, and in particular the event of the incarnation, relates to this natural sacred. Two contemporary thinkers suggest themselves for answering these questions, namely René Girard and Slavoj Žižek. Both authors defend in their work the uniqueness of Christianity and offer a Christology which is rooted in a non-Christian anthropology. If we want to trace down 'the uniqueness of Christianity' starting from the natural condition of humankind, this seems to hold great promise because it suggests that these authors will enable us to find arguments for this uniqueness without having to apply to the content of revelation. In the following chapters, we now examine whether the work of Girard and Žižek is indeed able to establish the uniqueness of Christianity.

# Chapter 2
# René Girard

## 1. Introducing René Girard

René Girard is a literary critic, historian and anthropologist. He was born in 1923 on Christmas day in Avignon (France). In 1947, he moved to the United States where he obtained a doctorate in history and taught at several universities (Indiana, Johns Hopkins, Buffalo, Stanford). He has developed a theory of religion and violence that is based on two elements, namely the imitative character of human desire and the victimage or scapegoating mechanism. The first element, the imitative character of human desire, was discovered by Girard through a study of literature and presented in his first book, *Mensonge romantique et vérité romanesque* (Romantic lie and novelistic truth), which was published in 1961.[1] In his second book, *La violence et le sacré* (Violence and the sacred), published in 1972,[2] Girard turned his attention to mythology, in this way discovering the violent origins of human culture. In 1978, he shocked his atheistic readers – who had been happy to adopt his work to discard all religion, including Christianity – by explicitly defending, in his *Des choses cachées depuis la fondation du monde* (Things hidden since the foundation of the world),[3] Christianity

---

[1] René Girard, *Mensonge romantique et vérité romanesque* (Paris: Editions Bernard Grasset, 1961). Translated into English as: *Deceit, Desire, and the Novel: Self and Other in Literary Structure* (trans. Yvonne Treccero; Baltimore, MD and London: The Johns Hopkins Press, 1965) (henceforth cited as *DDN*).

[2] René Girard, *La Violence et le sacré* (Paris: Editions Bernard Grasset, 1972). Translated into English as: *Violence and the Sacred* (trans. Patrick Gregory; London: The Athlone Press, 1995) (henceforth cited as *VS*).

[3] René Girard, *Des choses cachées depuis la fondation du monde* (Paris: Editions Grasset & Fasquelle, 1978). Translated into English as: *Things Hidden since the Foundation of the World* (research undertaken in collaboration with Jean-Michel Oughourlian and Guy Lefort; trans. Stephen Bann and Michael Metteer; London: The Athlone Press, 1987) (henceforth cited as *TH*).

as the revelation of these violent origins and therefore as a critique of the violence to which atheism itself still remains tributary. In this introduction we first discuss Girard's view of human desire as imitative and the victimage mechanism, before turning to a discussion of his Christology in the next section.

## a. Human Desire as Imitative

At the beginning of the first part of his *Things Hidden since the Foundation of the World*, René Girard stresses the importance of imitation (also called 'mimicry' or 'mimesis') for all human culture. Girard writes that 'There is nothing, or next to nothing, in human behaviour that is not learned, and all learning is based on imitation. If human beings suddenly ceased imitating, all forms of culture would vanish' (*TH* 7). The central role played by imitation was also already present in *Deceit, Desire, and the Novel*. In this book, Girard claims that the *romanesque* oeuvre – the novels of Miguel de Cervantes, Gustav Flaubert, Stendhal, Marcel Proust, and Fyodor Dostoyevsky – reveal the basic fact that human desire is always based on imitating a model. As a result, desire is always triangular. Our desire for a certain object is always aroused by an other who directs our attention to that particular object. It is the other's desire that makes an object desirable. This can easily be seen in kindergarten. Give a number of children each an identical toy and nonetheless they will soon start quarrelling because the toy of another child always looks more promising than the one they have. This triangular character of desire is the novelistic truth which refutes the romantic belief in the autonomy and spontaneity of desire. Or as Girard puts it:

> The romantic *vaniteux* always wants to convince himself
> that his desire is written into the nature of things, or,
> which amounts to the same thing, that it is the emanation
> of a serene subjectivity, the creation *ex nihilo* of a quasi-
> divine ego (*DDN* 15).[4]

[4] As can be deduced from this quotation, Girard does not use inclusive language. In order not to hide Girard's biased language, I have chosen not to alter quotations taken from his work. In the rest of the text, however, inclusive language has been adopted, because I am convinced that Girard's basic insight into the mimetic character of human desire is true for both sexes.

In the aforementioned novels, Girard also finds a shift from an external to an internal mediation of desire. In the case of *external mediation*, the distance between subject and model prevents their becoming competitors of each other. For instance, the model of Don Quixote is Amadis of Gaul, who, being a figure from the romances of chivalry he reads, can never become a real threat for Don Quixote. The same applies for Sancho, Don Quixote's servant, whose model is Don Quixote, but since Sancho and his master are clearly separated through boundaries of class, they do not become rivals. *Internal mediation*, on the other hand, comes into being when the distance to the model becomes smaller. As this distance grows smaller, the model increasingly becomes a rival. The subject and the model become competitors for the same object and the model appears, to an increasing extent, as an obstacle preventing the obtainment of the desired object (*DDN* 7–9).

This triangular desire is also discussed by Girard in *Violence and the Sacred*. In this book the role played by the model/rival is put as follows:

> In all the varieties of desire examined by us, we have encountered not only a subject and an object but a third presence as well: the rival. It is the rival who should be accorded the dominant role. . . . The rival desires the same object as the subject, and to assert the primacy of the rival can lead to only one conclusion. Rivalry does not arise because of the fortuitous convergence of two desires on one single object; rather, *the subject desires the object because the rival desires it*. In desiring an object the rival alerts the subject to the desirability of the object. The rival, then, serves as a model for the subject, not only in regard to such secondary matters as style and opinions but also, and more essentially, in regard to desires (*VS* 145).

In this way, it becomes clear that the object of desire is only of secondary importance. Or, as Girard puts it in *Deceit, Desire, and the Novel*, 'The object is only a means of reaching the mediator. The desire is aimed at the mediator's *being*.' It is '[t]he desire to absorb the being of the mediator' (*DDN* 53). The same idea is also put forward in *Violence and the Sacred*, where Girard describes the human animal as a creature that is characterized by a lack of being, a being that she or he descries in the other who serves as his or her model. That model seems to possess the secret of being and directs the desire of the subject to an object that appears as being capable to give that supreme plenitude of being:

> [Man] desires *being*, something he himself lacks and which some other person seems to possess. The subject thus looks to that other person to inform him of what he should desire in order to acquire that being. If the model, who is apparently already endowed with superior being, desires some object, that object must surely be capable of conferring an even greater plenitude of being. It is not through words, therefore, but by the example of his own desire that the model conveys to the subject the supreme desirability of the object (*VS* 146).

So, in fact, the desiring subject aims at stealing 'from the mediator his [or her] very being' and thus 'wants to become the Other', while, simultaneously, still remaining him/herself (*DDN* 54; see also p. 83: 'Imitative desire is always a desire to be Another'). The object is only a means to reach that goal.

Since, as Girard claims, our desires are always copied from a model, simply by desiring, we always and inevitably come into conflict with the model of our desires. This is especially visible, as already indicated above, in the case of internal mediation. As long as the model remains at a safe distance, the link between the model and particular objects is loose. Or, as Girard puts it with regard to Don Quixote, a 'distant mediator sheds a diffuse light over a vast surface. Amadis does not indicate precisely any particular object of desire, but on the other hand he designates vaguely almost everything.' For this reason, Don Quixote is not stubbornly attached to one particular object and quickly directs his desire to another object in the case of a setback. However, as the distance between subject and model grows smaller, the information of the model on what object to desire becomes more precise. Ultimately, the subject's desire is directed to one particular object, which increasingly becomes irreplaceable, and from which the complete fullness of being is expected. But while in this way the supreme plenitude of being seemingly has become within reach of the subject, it simultaneously remains all the more inaccessible. For, the model, who also desires that same object, blocks the way, becoming an obstacle, preventing the subject to reach the desired object (*DDN* 84–85).

This does not take away, however, that the object is still of only secondary importance. Moreover, as desire increasingly focuses on one particular object from which the fullness of being is expected, the practical value of the object in question becomes irrelevant.[5] The desired object is invested with a value far beyond its physical characteristics and can be said to achieve a 'metaphysical' status. This elevated position of the desired object explains the disappointment when the hero, after a great deal of effort, finally succeeds in obtaining the object. Its metaphysical aura immediately evaporates and all there is left is an ordinary object.[6] Though this result is, according to Girard, 'irrefutable proof of the absurdity of triangular desire' (*TH* 88–89), the subject is usually not prepared to admit this simple fact. He or she will seek a new object or will even resort to a new mediator.[7] But each object results, once obtained, in the same disappointment and as long as the subject does not give up her or his belief in acquiring the fullness of being through the possession of an object, it will remain the victim of an endless succession of mediators and/or objects; until finally he or she may eventually end up with desiring an object that is completely inaccessible, absolutely forbidden by a mediator. By doing so, the subject can both save his or her desire and protect him/herself from yet another disillusion. Girard puts this as follows:

[5] *DDN* 88: 'Even in the most favorable cases, the physical qualities of the object play only a subordinate role. They can neither rouse metaphysical desire nor prolong it; [. . .]'

[6] *DDN* 88: 'The subject discovers that possession of the object has not changed his being – the expected metamorphosis has not taken place.' See also:

The moment the hero takes hold of the desired object its "virtue" disappears like gas from a burst balloon. The object has been suddenly desecrated by possession and reduced to its objective qualities, thus provoking the famous Stendhalian exclamation: "Is that all it is?!" (*Ibid.*)

A man sets out to discover a treasure he believes is hidden under a stone; he turns over stone after stone but finds nothing. He grows tired of such a futile undertaking but the treasure is too precious for him to give up. So he begins to look for *a stone which is too heavy to lift* – he places all his hopes in that stone and he will waste all his remaining strength on it (*DDN* 176).

In this way, desire can ultimately even turn into 'a desire of the obstacle' (*DDN* 178).

As we shall see in what follows, Girard not only points out the role played in imitation by the model, but also teaches us the intimate link between imitation and conflict. In the next subsection we shall elaborate on this relation between imitation and conflict, and on the light it sheds on the origins of human culture.

## b. The Way from Imitation to Culture Passes through Violence

Human beings are imitating animals. But our discussion of Girard's view on desire in the previous subsection has exhibited that humans not only imitate each other's utensils and beliefs, but

---

[7] *DDN* 89–90:

> Two possibilities present themselves. The disillusioned hero can let his former mediator point out another object for him, or he can change mediators. The decision does not depend on "psychology" nor on "freedom", but, like so many other aspects of metaphysical desire, on the distance separating hero and mediator.
>
> When this distance is great, we know that the object has little metaphysical value. The prestige of the mediator is not involved in particular desires. The god is above the vicissitudes of existence. He is unique and eternal. Don Quixote has many adventures but there is only one Amadis; Mme Bovary could go on changing lovers endlessly without ever changing her dream. As the mediator draws near, the object is very closely linked with him and the god's divine image is at stake, so to speak. The failure of desire can now have repercussions beyond the object and provoke doubts concerning the mediator himself. At first the idol trembles on its pedestal; it may even collapse if the disillusionment is great enough.

also each other's desires (a phenomenon designated by Girard as 'acquisitive mimesis', the pursuit of precisely those objects which are desired by the imitated model). But, by doing so, humans come into conflict with each other. Since two people cannot both possess the same object, they become rivals of one another, competitors for the object they both desire. This clash of competing desires can easily turn into violence. For, if I can get rid of the other, I shall be able to conquer the object that will provide with the fullness of being. But, of course, the other thinks the same of me and in this way we can easily sink away in a spiral of reciprocal violence. From this intimate link between imitation and violence (through conflicting desires), we may conclude that, once our ancestors acquired the trick of imitation, the most important challenge they were confronted with was controlling the violence which arises from conflicting desires. This challenge is especially pressing because humankind seems to lack, as Girard indicates repeatedly, the protection of the 'braking mechanisms against violence' found among animals, which ensure that 'animals of the same species never fight to the death, but [that] the victor spares the life of the vanquished' (*VS* 221; see also already p. 145). Though the existence of such 'braking mechanisms' among animals is not uncontested by biologists,[8] it is nevertheless clear that culture provides humans with the possibility to be much more violent, cruel and efficient in killing; not only prey and predators, but also one's own species.

With the help of Girard's work, we can then make the following reconstruction of the origins of human culture. We may safely assume that an increasing ability to imitate went together with increasing acquisitive mimesis; resulting in more and more rivalry, aggression and violence within the early hominin group. Ever more frequently, the entire group became involved in a spiral of violence of all against all, a situation designated by Girard as the 'mimetic crisis'. During one of these crises, something

---

[8] See for instance: Richard Dawkins, *The Selfish Gene* (Oxford and New York, NY: Oxford University Press, new edn, 1989) p. 67. The 1989 edition of *The Selfish Gene* extends the 1976 edition with two extra chapters. The original text, however, is reprinted unaltered; though commented upon in endnotes.

unexpected happened: in the tumult one hominin, by accident, killed a fellow:

> There is yet some commotion. But no, [the victim]
> does not move anymore. He does nothing anymore.
> He does not hit back, but he does not surrender either.
> The other apes break off their fights and come to take
> a look. A circle is formed around the deceased. Silence.
> This is not possible. This is not in keeping with the
> scenario of the fight, which, up to now, was determined
> by instinctive rules . . . Only little by little, the circle around
> the deceased dissolves and the apes return to their daily
> pursuits.

This course of events was repeated each time when mimesis culminated in a mimetic crisis, in reciprocal violence of all against all:

> Time after time, the same happens. There is total disorder,
> a lot of aggression and violence; and suddenly, suddenly
> someone is killed. Violence stops, and everybody comes to
> take a look at the deceased. They form a circle. Suddenly,
> disorder disappears and an ordered structure comes into
> being: a circle around the deceased. Moreover, disorder
> and violence do not return immediately. The circle
> dissolves, and the apes take up again their daily routine.
> Rest has come back in the group.

After numerous repetitions of this same course of events, the hominins began to recognize a certain structure: they learned that killing an individual puts a stop to the mimetic crisis. In this way, the victimage mechanism came into being. Or, to put it differently, the scapegoat was born.[9]

---

[9] This paragraph is based on the summary of *Violence and the Sacred* offered by Jan Populier in his *God heeft echt bestaan: Met René Girard naar een nieuw mens- en wereldbeeld* (Tielt [W.-Vl.]: Lannoo – Mimesis, 1994) pp. 18–21 (the translation of both quotations is mine).

As Girard demonstrates in *Violence and the Sacred* and also in the first chapter of *Things Hidden since the Foundation of the World*, scapegoating is the basis of human civilization. Since any group of humans always runs the risk of being engulfed by a mimetic crisis, which sweeps away every individual in a spiral of rivalry, reciprocal violence and aggression, human culture can only last when this mimetic crisis is suppressed by killing a scapegoat. As Jan Populier stresses in his discussion of the scapegoating mechanism, the scapegoat appears as highly ambivalent. On the one hand, since with his/her death violence comes to a stop, s/he is held responsible for that violence and, as such, considered as evil. On the other hand, however, s/he is also the one who, by dying, delivers the community of violence and, therefore, appears as a rescuer (and thus as good). Populier puts this ambivalence as follows:

> All evil, violence and disorder are in [the scapegoat].
> All recovered rest, order and peace are in him as well.
> He transcends every physically perceptible thing. He is
> the very first metaphysical phenomenon. Being the
> embodiment of all evil, violence and disorder, his return
> to society must be prevented at all costs. He must disappear,
> must be removed from society once and for all. For, in case
> he would stand up and start to fight again, society will fall
> back into violence. As the embodiment of all goodness, rest
> and order, however, he must also remain present in society.
> He must be present permanently in order to guarantee rest
> and order in society.

As a result, the scapegoat becomes a supernatural being that decides on peace and violence, order and disorder, good and evil. As the source of violence, s/he should be feared; as the source of peace, however, s/he should be worshipped. In this way, according to Girard, the primitive godhead is born. Or, as Populier puts it, the scapegoat calls into being the metaphysical, the sacred, the divine.[10]

---

[10] Populier, *God heeft echt bestaan*, p. 23 (the translation of the quotation is mine).

Gradually, moreover, the hominins increasingly learn to antici-pate the mimetic crisis. They no longer passively wait until yet another mimetic crisis engulfs their community, but they simulate such a crisis and kill a victim in order to *prevent* violence. In this way, the feast comes into being, a feast in which the mimetic crisis is enacted and which is then concluded with a sacrifice. In *Things Hidden since the Foundation of the World*, Girard designates this as 'the imperative of ritual'. Furthermore, rules will be laid down in order to discourage acquisitive mimesis. This is designated by Girard as 'the imperative of prohibition' (*TH* 28). In this way, both rituals and taboos (and actually human culture in general) can be understood as a defence against violence.

Against this background, we are now able to understand Girard's Christological reflections.

## 2. Girard's Christology: Christ Reveals the Violent Foundations of Culture

### a. Girard's Account of the Christ Event

According to Girard, the Bible tells us the story of a gradual exit from mythological religion. This disclosure already began in the third chapter of Genesis with the story of Cain and Abel. At first sight, this story is as mythological as, for instance, the story on Remus and Romulus: one out of two brothers murders the other and a civilization/city is founded. There is however an important difference between both stories. While in the Roman myth, the action is considered as justified by Remus's violation of the ideal border of the new city laid down by Romulus, the Bible unam-biguously condemns Cain's act towards his brother as an unjusti-fied and vulgar murder (*TH* 146–47). Another example can be found in the story on Joseph. In that story, Joseph denounces the advances made to him by the wife of his Egyptian master, but is subsequently accused by her of having attempted to seduce her and is thrown in prison. This story has a clear parallel in the Greek story of Hippolytus and his young stepmother Phaedra. The former offends Aphrodite by his excessive chastity and the god-dess reacts by instigating a crush for Hippolytus in Phaedra.

Hippolytus reacts with horror and rejection to the advances by Phaedra, who responds to the rejection by killing herself, but not without leaving a letter for her husband Theseus (Hippolytus's father) in which she falsely accuses him of having tried to rape her. Theseus curses his son and utters the wish that he would die, something which happens when on the same day Hippolytus's horses bolt after they are frightened by a monster raising from the sea. Though both stories share a similar plot, there is nevertheless an important difference between them: the Bible presents Joseph as an innocent victim, while the Greek myth implies that Hippolytus, though not guilty in the modern sense, has nevertheless been punished rightly for his excessive chastity, which amounts to hubris and offends Aphrodite (*TH* 152). By disclosing in this way the innocence of the victim, the Bible undermined the mythological-sacrificial order, which was precisely based on the belief in the guiltiness of the victim:

> Myths incorporate the point of view of the
> community that has been reconciled to itself by the
> collective murder and is unanimously convinced that
> this event was a legitimate and sacred action, desired by
> God himself, which could not conceivably be repudiated,
> criticized, or analysed (*TH* 148).

The Bible, in contrast, by choosing the side of the victim, began to desacralize violence (*TH* 153).

In addition to its undermining of mythology, the Bible also subverted the two other pillars of primitive religion, namely the sacrificial order and the obsession with divinely ordained rules (which both had to prevent a resurgence of the mimetic crisis). In both subversions, the Prophets played a decisive role with their rejection of sacrifices and legalism (see, for instance, Hos. 6.6: 'For I desire steadfast love and not sacrifice, the knowledge of God rather than burnt-offerings.'). In the Hebrew Bible, Girard sees this critique of primitive religion culminating in a fragment from the fourth of the so-called *Songs of the Servant of the Lord* (Isa. 53.2–10):

> 2 For he grew up before him like a young plant,
> and like a root out of dry ground;

he had no form or majesty that we should look at him,
nothing in his appearance that we should desire him.

3 He was despised and rejected by others;
a man of suffering and acquainted with infirmity;
and as one from whom others hide their faces
he was despised, and we held him of no account.

4 Surely he has borne our infirmities
and carried our diseases;
yet we accounted him stricken,
struck down by God, and afflicted.

5 But he was wounded for our transgressions,
crushed for our iniquities;
upon him was the punishment that made us whole,
and by his bruises we are healed.

6 All we like sheep have gone astray;
we have all turned to our own way,
and the Lord has laid on him
the iniquity of us all.

7 He was oppressed, and he was afflicted,
yet he did not open his mouth;
like a lamb that is led to the slaughter,
and like a sheep that before its shearers is silent,
so he did not open his mouth.

8 By a perversion of justice he was taken away.
Who could have imagined his future?
For he was cut off from the land of the living,
stricken for the transgression of my people.

9 They made his grave with the wicked
and his tomb with the rich,
although he had done no violence,
and there was no deceit in his mouth.

10 Yet it was the will of the Lord to crush him with pain.
When you make his life an offering for sin,
he shall see his offspring, and shall prolong his days;
through him the will of the Lord shall prosper.

According to Girard, this fragment begins by describing the Servant of the Lord as the ideal sacrificial victim (Verses 2 and 3). He is characterized in similarity with the Greek *phármakos*, a scapegoat which was chosen on the basis of his ugliness or uncanny appearance. Yet, the text makes it clear that we are not dealing with a ritual sacrifice, but with 'a spontaneous historical event, which has at once a collective and a legal character, and is sanctioned by the authorities' (Verse 8: 'By a perversion of justice he was taken away'). Moreover, the innocence of the victim is explicitly proclaimed (Verse 7: the Servant does not resist, he is like a lamb, like a sheep; and Verse 9: he is without violence, without deceit). In addition to the innocence of the victim, the guiltiness of the community is stressed: the Servant died because of 'our transgressions', 'our iniquities' (Verse 5, see also Verse 6). Furthermore, though not explicitly mentioned by Girard while discussing this fragment, the positive impact of violence for the community is also recognized (Verse 4 and 6: by taking up our pain and bearing our suffering, the Servant has brought us peace and healing; or, to put it differently: this fragment describes the scapegoating mechanism). But, as Girard notes, though this text goes a long way in unearthing the victimage mechanism, it is not able to bring the desacralization of violence to its end. For, though Verse 4 seems to reluctantly introduce a critique of the belief that violence is divinely ordained ('*we accounted* him stricken, struck down by God, and afflicted'), Verse 10 greatly reconfirms the view that God wills the death of his Servant for the well-being of his people ('Yet it was the will of the Lord to crush him with pain'). Thus, in the Hebrew Bible, Girard concludes, God remains contaminated by violence (*TH* 154–57).[11]

---

[11] See also p. 158, where Jean-Michel Oughourlian, one of the two of Girard's interlocutors in *Things Hidden* (which is written under the form of a dialogue), summarizes the achievement of the Hebrew Bible as follows:

The myths are worked through with a form of inspiration that runs counter to them, but they continue in being. The sacrifices are criticized, but they continue; the law is simplified and declared to be identical to the love of one's neighbour, but it continues. And even though he is presented in a less and less violent form, and becomes more and more benevolent, Yahweh it still the god to whom vengeance belongs. The notion of divine retribution is still alive.

In Girard's view, the desacralization of violence, begun in the first chapters of the Hebrew Bible, found its completion in the Gospels, in which God was purged from all violence, which was unmasked as a merely human phenomenon. In this regard, Girard refers in particular to the command to love one's enemy,[12] but also to the identification of God with love (found in the Johannine corpus) and to the texts in which God's responsibility for infirmity, illness and catastrophes is denied (*TH* 182–83). Moreover, the Gospels do not offer a sacrificial interpretation of Jesus' death on the cross (in the sense that God would need a bloody sacrifice to satisfy his offended honour), the Apocalypse, of which Jesus holds out the prospect, does not concern God's violence and Jesus does not ascribe any violence to God in his parables (*TH* 185–89). Much of this will probably sound counterintuitive to many Christians. Indeed, Christ's Crucifixion has traditionally been understood in sacrificial terms, Apocalypse has been considered as a violent interruption of God in history and also God's violence in the parables has been noted (see, for instance, the parable of the murderous tenants of the vineyard and the parable of the talents, in which Jesus seems to hold out the prospect of divine retribution).

In order to appreciate Girard's claims, we should keep in mind that he identifies Satan as 'the principle of all human community', 'the circular mechanisms of violence', and as 'man's imprisonment in cultural or philosophical systems that maintain his *modus vivendi* with violence' (*TH* 162). According to Girard, humankind is subjected to the power of violence. Humans are inhabitants of the kingdom of Satan, captives of violence. Jesus proclaimed another Kingdom, the Kingdom of God, which implies 'the complete and definitive elimination of every form of vengeance and every form of reprisal in relations between men. Jesus offered his listeners the chance to escape from the kingdom of Satan and to enter the

---

[12] Cf. Mt. 5.43–45:

You have heard that it was said, 'You shall love your neighbour and hate your enemy.' But I say to you, Love your enemies and pray for those who persecute you, so that you may be children of your Father in heaven; for he makes his sun rise on the evil and on the good, and sends rain on the righteous and on the unrighteous.

Kingdom of God. He invited everybody to renounce violence, to leave it behind, by giving up the idea of retribution. This entails, however, that certain forms of conduct, which had until then been considered as legitimate, had to be abandoned (see in this regard the Sermon on the Mount). Or, as Girard puts it:

> We think it quite fair to respond to good dealings with good dealings, and to evil dealings with evil, but this is precisely what all the communities on the planet have always done, with familiar results. People imagine that to escape from violence it is sufficient to give up any kind of violent *initiative*, but since no one in fact thinks of himself as taking this initiative – since all violence has a mimetic character, and derives or can be thought to derive from a first violence that is always perceived as originating with the opponent – this act of renunciation is no more than a sham, and cannot bring about any change at all. Violence is always perceived as being a legitimate reprisal or even self-defence. So what must be given up is the right to reprisals and even the right to what passes, in a number of cases, for legitimate defence.

Thus, in Girard's view, the Gospel doctrine is 'good news' because it gives us all we need to know in order to escape from violence. The only thing which is needed in order to let the Kingdom of God come is that humankind as a whole, and each individual separately, renounces vengeance (*TH* 196–99).

Jesus' message was not accepted, however. His listeners were so blinded by their attachment to violence that they were not even able to understand him. As a result, 'the direct and easy way' out of violence failed, namely that all would accept the principles proclaimed by Jesus in the Sermon on the Mount. Therefore, it became 'necessary to turn to the indirect way, the one that has to bypass the consent of all mankind and instead passes through the Crucifixion and the Apocalypse'. Thus, in Girard's view, the Crucifixion became inevitable and the proclamation of Jesus became apocalyptic only *after* his initial proclamation of the Kingdom remained unsuccessful. This, Girard adds, is not to repeat the nineteenth-century view that Jesus' 'apocalyptic turn' resulted from bitterness because his message was not accepted and should be understood 'as an appeal to the anger of God' (*TH* 202–03). On the contrary, his Crucifixion is the inevitable outcome of the already established sacrificial logic. Once his message had been turned down, Jesus was bound to become its victim (*TH* 208). For, in a world dominated by violence, one can only survive by becoming accessory to violence. Jesus, however, was and remained without violence. But somebody untainted by violence can only become its victim (*TH* 210–11), and by becoming in this way a victim, Jesus exposed the violent foundations of human culture. Because he was without violence, it is clear that he cannot be guilty and that his death is a huge injustice. In this way, the Crucifixion reveals what has been hidden since the foundation of the world (cf. Mt. 13.35), namely that each human community is based on the killing or expulsion of innocent victims (*TH* 209).[13] In this way, Jesus showed humankind its true destiny, its true vocation: to rid itself from captivity by violence.

All this brings Girard to subscribing to the divinity of Christ and the doctrine of the incarnation, for the truth about violence can only be brought to light by someone who is not held captive by violence. Yet, such a person cannot be generated by a world completely dominated by violence. Consequently, the only logical conclusion is that Jesus was not an ordinary human being, but God incarnate (*TH* 218–19).

## b. Girard vs. Nietzsche: Dionysus and the Crucified One

'Have I been understood? – *Dionysus versus* [German: *gegen*, 'against'] *the crucified.*' This is the last sentence of *Ecce Homo: How One Becomes What One Is*, one of the last works completed by

---

[13] See *TH* 209:

> What violence does not and cannot comprehend is that, in getting rid of Jesus by the usual means, it falls into a trap that could only be laid by innocence of such a kind because it is not really a trap: there is nothing hidden. Violence reveals its own game in such a way that its workings are compromised at their very source; the more it tries to conceal its ridiculous secret from now on, by forcing itself into action, the more it will succeed in revealing itself.

Nietzsche before his mental collapse on January 3, 1889 ('Why I Am a Destiny', §9).[14] The opposition between Dionysus and the Crucified is most extensively discussed in an aphorism from the *Nachlass*. This aphorism, which dates from the spring of 1888, is entitled *The Two Types: Dionysus and the Crucified One* and in it we read the following:

> Dionysos versus the 'Crucified One': there you have the opposition. It's *not* a distinction regarding their martyrdom – just that this martyrdom has a different meaning. Life itself, its eternal fruitfulness and recurrence, conditions torment, destruction, the will to annihilation . . .
>
> in the other case suffering, 'the Crucified as the innocent', counts as an objection to this life, a formula to condemn it.
>
> One divines that the problem here is that of the meaning of suffering: whether a Christian meaning, a tragic meaning . . . In the former case it's held to be the path to a blissful existence; in the latter, *existence* is held to be *blissful enough* to justify even monstrous suffering
>
> The tragic man says Yes to even the bitterest suffering: he is strong, full, deifying enough to do so
>
> The Christian says No to even the happiest earthly lot: he is weak, poor, disinherited enough to suffer from life in whatever form . . .
>
> 'the God on the cross' is a curse on life, a hint to deliver oneself from it
>
> Dionysos cut to pieces is a *promise* to life: it will eternally be reborn and come home out of destruction.[15]

[14] See: Friedrich Nietzsche, *The Anti-Christ, Ecce Homo, Twilight of the Idols and Other Writings* (ed. Aaron Ridley and Judith Norman; trans. Judith Norman; Cambridge Texts in the History of Philosophy; Cambridge: Cambridge University Press, 2005) p. 151 (henceforth cited as *AC/EH*).

[15] Friedrich Nietzsche, *Writings from the Late Notebooks* (ed. Rüdiger Bittner; trans. Kate Sturge; Cambridge Texts in the History of Philosophy; Cambridge: Cambridge University Press, 2003) pp. 249–50 (= *KGW* VIII, 3:14 [§89]) (henceforth cited as *WLN*).

Girard discusses this fragment in an article from 1984,[16] in which he uses it to clarify the uniqueness of Christianity. This is less strange than it may seem at first sight. For, 'unlike most of his contemporaries and ours', Girard states, 'Nietzsche strongly believed in the unique specificity of the Biblical and Christian perspective'. This is important because, as Girard notes, Nietzsche's 'reasons cannot be dismissed as summarily as they would if he were a Christian' (*DVC* 818 [246]). In this, Girard and Nietzsche agree. But they are diametrically opposed in their evaluation of both sides of the opposition. Nietzsche professes himself a disciple of Dionysus,[17] while Girard sides with the Crucified One. In what follows, we shall first discuss the opposition between Dionysus and the Crucified as it appears in Nietzsche's thought, before turning to Girard's evaluation of Nietzsche.

### b.1. Nietzsche: Dionysus Against the Crucified One

As indicated by Paul Valadier in his *Jésus-Christ ou Dionysos*, Nietzsche is using 'Dionysus' and 'the Crucified One' as symbols for two types of human beings, for two ways of relating to the world and to oneself.[18] In order to understand this opposition, we have to know who Dionysus was for Nietzsche. In this regard, Valadier warns against deriving the meaning Dionysus had for Nietzsche from a study of Greek mythology.[19] Indeed, when, in *Ecce Homo*, he is looking back upon *The Birth of Tragedy* (1872), in which he had introduced the distinction between 'the Apollonian' and 'the Dionysian', Nietzsche attributes his discovery of 'the amazing phenomenon of the Dionysian' to his 'own innermost

---

[16] René Girard, 'Dionysus versus the Crucified', *MLN* 99/4 (1984), pp. 816–35. Republished in James G. Williams (ed.), *The Girard Reader* (repr., New York, NY: Crossroad Publishing, 2003) pp. 243–61. In what follows, we shall refer to the original version, but shall mention the corresponding pages of the 2003-version between square brackets. Henceforth cited as *DVC*.

[17] See, for instance: *Ecce Homo*, 'Preface', §2 (*AC/EH* 71): 'I am a disciple of the philosopher Dionysus'. (On Dionysus as philosopher, see below.)

[18] Paul Valadier, *Jésus-Christ ou Dionysos: La foi chrétienne en confrontation avec Nietzsche* (Jésus et Jésus-Christ, 10; Paris: Desclée, 1979) pp. 230–31.

[19] See already: Paul Valadier, *Nietzsche et la critique du christianisme* (Cogitatio fidei, 77; Paris: Les Editions du Cerf, 1974) p. 554.

experience' and adds that he was 'the first person ever' who understood it (*Ecce Homo*, 'The Birth of Tragedy', §2).[20] Thus, in order
to unearth the meaning of Nietzsche's Dionysus, we should not
turn to Greek mythology, but proceed by a careful reading of
Nietzsche himself.

Such a reading is offered by Valadier in the last chapter of
his *Nietzsche et la critique du christianisme*. As Valadier points out,
Nietzsche characterizes his Dionysus as both God and as philosopher. With regard to the second characteristic, Valadier refers to
§295 of *Beyond Good and Evil*, where Nietzsche writes 'that
Dionysus is a philosopher, and that gods too therefore philoso-
phize'.[21] From the fact that Nietzsche characterizes Dionysus as
philosopher, Valadier draws the conclusion that the Nietzschean
Dionysian cannot be identified with 'an irrational and unbridled
ecstasy', but should be linked to knowledge, and to Nietzsche's
'gay science' in particular.[22] In the aforementioned section from
*Ecce Homo* ('The Birth of Tragedy', §2), knowledge (*Erkenntniss*)
and an affirmative stance towards life ('*das Jasagen zur Realität*')
are even identified.[23] Yet, even if Dionysus is a philosopher, he is
not a philosopher like Socrates, the prototype of the 'theoretical
man', who derails life by opposing instinct and/with reason. In
this way, 'Socrates' is a name for 'the *degenerate* instinct that turns
against life with subterranean vindictiveness', while 'Dionysus' is
a name for 'the *highest affirmation* born out of fullness, out of
overfullness, and unreserved yea-saying even to suffering, even to
guilt, even to everything questionable and strange about existence'
(*AC/EH* 109). The philosophy of Dionysus is an affirmative
philosophy.[24]

[20] *AC/EH* 108; as mentioned in Valadier, *Nietzsche*, p. 553 and *Jésus-Christ ou Dionysos*, p. 237 (n. 6).
[21] See: Friedrich Nietzsche, *Beyond Good and Evil: Prelude to a Philosophy of the Future* (trans. R.J. Hollingdale; intr. Michael Tanner; Penguin Classics; repr. with rev. and new introd., London: Penguin Books, 1990) p. 220.
[22] See: Valadier, *Nietzsche*, p. 556.
[23] 'Knowledge, saying yes to reality is [. . .]' (*AC/EH* 109). See also, in the same section: 'This final, most joyful, effusive, high-spirited yes to life is not only the highest insight, it is also the most *profound*, the most rigorously confirmed and supported by truth and study.'
[24] Cf. Valadier, *Nietzsche*, pp. 556–58.

If Dionysus as affirmative philosopher is opposed by Nietzsche to Socrates, Dionysus in his capacity as a god is, as we have already seen in the fragment from the *Nachlass* quoted above, opposed to the Crucified One.[25] This opposition should not be understood as if the Crucified stands for a morbid fascination by and obsession with suffering and death, while Dionysus would symbolize a rejection of suffering. Nietzsche's Dionysian does not entail a neglect of the painful side of life. On the contrary, Dionysus is both 'sensuality and cruelty', 'engendering and destroying' (*WLN* 79 = *KGW* VIII,1:2[§106]), 'creating and annihilating' (*WLN* 81 = *KGW* VIII,1:2[§10]). Moreover, in a fragment from the autumn of 1887, Nietzsche writes that he 'aspired to a justification of life, even in its most dreadful, ambiguous and mendacious forms' and therefore he coined 'the formula "Dionysian"' (*WLN* 149 = *KGW* VIII,2:9[§44]). The opposition between Dionysus and the Crucified One is thus as indicated in the fragment quoted above *not*, 'a distinction regarding their martyrdom'. Indeed, like the Crucified, Dionysus also dies; he is even cut into pieces.[26]

The difference between both types concerns an opposing evaluation, a conflicting interpretation of suffering and death. The Crucified One stands for the ascetic ideal, the ideal of the weak, of the 'slaves', who feel threatened by life and try to escape from it by fleeing to a *Hinterwelt*. They attempt to subject life to a meaning or aim beyond it, but in this way, Nietzsche claims, they pervert the problem of its meaning. The Dionysian ideal, in contrast, entails an identification with life, as it is, and this even, as we have just seen, 'in its most dreadful, ambiguous and mendacious forms'. The Dionysian person does not search for a meaning of life beyond life, but says 'Yes!' to it, even if it chastises him/her with suffering and death, because s/he is convinced of life's overabundance and creative power. Or, as the fragment quoted above puts it, 'it will eternally be reborn and come home out of destruction'. While the weak freeze up life in fixed structures (eternal being), the strong, the masters, are able to affirm 'a becoming which is

---

[25] See: Valadier, *Nietzsche*, p. 558.
[26] Valadier, *Nietzsche*, p. 569; *Jésus-Christ ou Dionysos*, p. 233.

actively grasped, subjectively experienced, as a raging volu-
ptuousness of the creative man who also knows the wrath of the
destroyer' (*WLN* 81 =*KGW* VIII, 1:2[§110]). To sum up: the
Dionysian person, by affirming life, aspires at overcoming him/
herself, while the weak, by denying life, remain imprisoned by
their old subjectivity.[27]

By the way, it is remarkable that Nietzsche – who has proclaimed, through the madman of aphorism no. 125 of *The Gay
Science*, the death of God – opposes the old religious ideal (exem-
plified by the Crucified One) with a new *religious* ideal (symbolized
by Dionysus). In the aphorism on the two types, Nietzsche pleads
for 'the religious affirmation of life, of life as a whole, not denied
and halved' (*WLN* 249 = *KGW* VIII, 3:14[§ 89]). This makes
clear that Nietzsche was essentially a religious thinker, a fact which
both Valadier and Girard stress, and that his philosophy is not
essentially anti-religious, though it is anti-Christian.[28] Moreover,
as Girard notes, Nietzsche's polemic against Christianity became
even more intense as the years passed by. 'We cannot doubt', Girard
writes, 'that the closer we get to the end the more obsessive the
Christian theme becomes with Nietzsche' (*DVC* 818 [246]). In
this regard, we can for instance refer to his *The Anti-Christ:
A Curse on Christianity*, in which his attack on the religion of the
Crucified One reaches an embittered culmination point.

### b.2. Girard: The Crucified One Against Dionysus

Girard interprets Nietzsche's Dionysus as 'a single symbol . . . for
countless mythological cults' and he reads the phrase 'Dionysus
cut to pieces', from the aphorism on the two types quoted above,
as a reference to the mythological narrative according to which
Dionysus was ripped into pieces by the Titans (*DVC* 820–21
[248]). In this way, Girard seems to do exactly what Valadier
warned us against, namely trying to understand Nietzsche's
Dionysus starting from Greek mythology. Moreover, though he
admits that Nietzsche never analysed Euripides's *The Bacchantes*,

---

[27] See: Valadier, *Nietzsche*, pp. 566–68 and 569–70; *Jésus-Christ ou Dionysos*,
    p. 234.
[28] Valadier, *Jésus-Christ ou Dionysos*, pp. 229–30; *DVC* 816–18 [244–46].

Girard also links Nietzsche's Dionysian to the phenomenon of the Bacchanalia, while Valadier explicitly rejects such a link.[29] Though it is true, as Girard notes, that Nietzsche did not consider the Dionysian 'something idyllic and inconsequential' and that he was aware of its 'disturbing' and 'ugly sides', Girard's claim that Nietzsche 'always dutifully mentioned the Dionysian violence' (*DVC* 819 [247]) seems, at least on the basis of the study of Nietzsche's Dionysus presented above, less justified. And when Girard proceeds by adding that 'Nietzsche clearly saw that pagan mythology, like pagan ritual, centres on the killing of victims or on their expulsion' (*DVC* 819 [247]), it seems to become clear that Girard is reading too much of his own theory into Nietzsche.

Yet, irrespective of whether Girard is right about the fact that Nietzsche was aware of the link between his Dionysian ideal and violence, or not, it remains the case, at least in Girard's view, that choosing for Dionysus against the Crucified implies a return to sacral violence. This return of violence, Girard claims, can already be discerned in the work of Nietzsche himself:

> Hundreds of texts can be quoted that show beyond all doubt that Nietzsche's fierce stubbornness in opposing the inspiration of the Bible in favor of victims, logically and inexorably led him toward the more and more inhuman attitudes of his later years which he espoused, in words of course rather than in deeds, with a fortitude worthy of a better cause.

According to Girard, Nietzsche is the most perfect example of a trend found in general amongst intellectuals since the latter part of the eighteenth century, namely 'the inner compulsion . . . to adopt inhuman standards' (*DVC* 825 [252]). To explain this tendency, Girard falls back on Nietzsche's category of *ressentiment*, but not without using it against him. As Nietzsche indicates in *On the Genealogy of Morals: A Polemic*, slaves are not able to take revenge

[29] 'When [Nietzsche's] Dionysus is thus a God, his cult does engage neither in an unbridled bacchanal nor in madness of the senses: the God-philosopher wakens a disciple which can give himself the title of "*ein Wissender*"' (Valadier, *Nietzsche*, p. 557; my translation).

for what is done to them by their masters. Therefore, they have to interiorize that revenge, which turns it into *ressentiment*.[30] In Nietzsche's view, Christianity is a child of this *ressentiment*.[31] For Girard, however, Nietzsche was wrong about this: *ressentiment* is not the father of Christianity, but its child (*DVC* 825 [252]). To understand this claim of Girard, we have to take into account his evaluation of the history of Christianity.

Since people at the time of Jesus were living within the frame of sacrificial religion, for them Christ's death on the cross could not but appear as another sacrifice. It should not come as a surprise then that the first Christians quickly turned to a sacrificial interpretation of the Crucifixion (see, for instance, the Epistle to the Hebrews). Especially when Christianity entered the pagan world, which had, in contrast to the Jews, not been prepared by the 'demystifying effect' of the Hebrew Scriptures, a sacrificial Christianity became inevitable. This resulted in a 'resacralization': God was 'reinfused with violence'. In this regard, Girard speaks about a 'regression' to the Old Testament (and in particular to the *Songs of the Servant of the Lord*, which, as we have seen above, remain faithful to the idea of a violent God) (*TH* 224–27). The sacrificial interpretation of Jesus' death enabled the foundation of 'something that in principle [the Christian text] ought never to have founded', namely a new culture, a *Christian* culture, with a new sacrificial order and new scapegoats (such as Jews and witches). Paradoxically, precisely this distortion of the meaning of the Crucifixion explains its ultimate success. For, as Girard writes, the 'awe-inspiring spread of the Gospel could only [take] place with[in] the terms of the sacrificial reading'. Thus, only by becoming a new sacrificial religion, Christianity was able to be successful

---

[30] See: Friedrich Nietzsche, *On the Genealogy of Morals/Ecce Homo* (trans. Walter Kaufmann and R. J. Hollingdale; New York, NY: Vintage Books, 1989) p. 36: 'The slave revolt in morality begins when *ressentiment* itself becomes creative and gives birth to values: the *ressentiment* of natures that are denied the true reaction, that of deeds, and compensate themselves with an imaginary revenge' (I §10).

[31] See: *AC/EH* 136, where Nietzsche speaks about 'the birth of Christianity out of the spirit of *ressentiment*' (in the section on 'The Genealogy of Morality').

among the pagan people which had not been educated by the Old Testament. As a result, the true, radical message of the Gospels could only come to light after a long detour. Or, as Girard puts it:

> The role of historical Christianity becomes necessary within an eschatological process that is governed by the Gospels – a history directed towards revealing the universal truth of human violence. But the process requires an almost limitless patience: many centuries must elapse before the subversive and shattering truth contained in the Gospels can be understood world-wide (*TH* 249–53).

This idea of Girard has been developed further by the Belgian philosopher Guido Vanheeswijck, who describes the impact of the Gospels on Western civilization as follows:

> The Christian narratives on peace and charity have for centuries made their rounds in old Europe, to the farthest corners of godforsaken villages. Even when these narratives were only able to get through to the most superficial layers of consciousness and even when their content was often repressed by institutional preoccupations, they still had as inevitable effect that a culture which could for centuries listen to these narratives and claimed to live from them, could not simultaneously proclaim and justify violence unproblematically. In this way, Western civilization, as intermediary of the Christian message, has unmistakably problematized violence.[32]

But, as Vanheeswijck adds, 'a kingdom of perfect peace and charity' has not yet come about.[33] It is in this context that we can appreciate Girard's interpretation of *ressentiment*:

---

[32] Guido Vanheeswijck, *Voorbij het onbehagen: Ressentiment en christendom* [Beyond discontent: Ressentiment and Christianity] (Leuven: Davidsfonds, 2002) p. 69 (my translation).

[33] Vanheeswijck, *Voorbij het onbehagen*, p. 70 (my translation).

*Ressentiment* flourishes in a world where real vengeance (Dionysus) has been weakened. The Bible and the gospels have diminished the violence of vengeance and turned it to *ressentiment* not because they originate in the latter but because their real target is vengeance in all its forms, and they have only succeeded in wounding vengeance, not in eliminating it. The gospels are indirectly responsible; we alone are directly responsible. *Ressentiment* is the manner in which the spirit of vengeance survives the impact of Christianity and turns the gospels to its own use (*DVC* 825 [252]).

Vanheeswijck traces the emergence of *ressentiment* back to the sixteenth century and lets it coincide with the transition from a pre-modern, religiously hierarchically ordered society (based on the victimage mechanism) to a modern, economically oriented, egalitarian society (based on *ressentiment*).[34] Traditional, pre-modern cultures were afraid of equality, because it reminded them of the reciprocal violence of the mimetic crisis. To keep this violence at bay, primitive societies had installed a sacrificial order with many provisions (taboos, sacred laws, hierarchical structures) to curb acquisitive mimesis, to avoid in this way any situation in which human beings could become each other's rivals. Modern society emerges when this fear for equality disappears and when equality even becomes an ideal. This transition from pre-modern to modern coincides with a shift from external to internal mediation as the dominant form of mediation of desire. This results, for the reasons outlined the previous section, in increasing rivalry and competition between human beings. The more society becomes egalitarian, the more envy, vanity, greed and ambition become widespread. Of course, these feelings have always been part of human constitution, but while traditional cultures considered them to be harmful and attempted to restrain them, modernity began to see them as neutral or even positive characteristics. In this regard, Vanheeswijck refers to the remarkable fact that, while for medieval men and women competition was sinful, by the eighteenth century, it had become the eminent bourgeois virtue;

---

[34] Vanheeswijck, *Voorbij het onbehagen*, p. 70.

envy being considered as something positive because it inspires one to diligence and hard work, and in this way it becomes the engine of the economy. In this way, envy turns out to be the foundation of the modern market economy. However, the increasing competition and growing feelings of envy, vanity and greed result in a growing 'discontent in culture' (an *Unbehagen in der Kultur*, to use the title of a late work of Freud), a discontent which is the source of an ever increasing amount of *ressentiment* in modern culture.[35]

This *ressentiment* reached a culmination point in the latter part of the nineteenth century. 'Nietzsche', Girard writes, 'suffers so much from it that he mistakes it for the original and primary form of vengeance. He sees *ressentiment* not merely as the child of Christianity which it certainly is but also as its father which it certainly is not' (*DVC* 825 [252]). Thus, Nietzsche's mistake was that he considered *ressentiment*, which he dissected with such great care, as the essence of Christianity, while it is the outcome of the unfinished impact of Christianity on world history.[36] As outlined by Vanheeswijck, Nietzsche detected *ressentiment* everywhere: not only in Christian morality, but also in its modern offshoots: humanism, socialism, democracy and the affluent society. According to Girard, Nietzsche's aversion to it – his *ressentiment* of *ressentiment* – was so strong that he even longed for a return of 'real vengeance as a cure for what seemed to him the worst of all possible fates', the pale *ressentiment* of the 'last men'. But as Girard notes, this longing for real vengeance is a luxury which can only be afforded in a society in which violence has already been curtailed by the impact of the Gospel message and in which real vengeance is no longer a real threat. But contemporary humans can no longer permit themselves such 'frivolity' since, according to Girard:

> Real vengeance is back among us in the shape of nuclear and other absolute weapons, reducing our planet to the size of a global primitive village, terrified once again by the possibility of unlimited bloodfeud. . . .

[35] Vanheeswijck, *Voorbij het onbehagen*, p. 89, p. 90, pp. 91–92 and pp. 95–96.
[36] Cf. Vanheeswijck, *Voorbij het onbehagen*, p. 70; *DVC* 825 [252].

Compared to this, *ressentiment* and other 19th century annoyances pale to insignificance, or rather their only significance is the increasing rage everywhere that turns *ressentiment* back into irrepressible vengeance and can unleash the unspeakable.

At more and more levels of reality, the urgency of the gospel message can no longer be disregarded with impunity. Those thinkers who, like Nietzsche, unthinkingly appealed to real vengeance in their itch to get rid of *ressentiment* resemble these foolish characters in fairytales who make the wrong wish and come to grief when it comes true (*DVC* 825–26 [253]).[37]

To conclude with Vanheeswijck: we may appreciate Nietzsche for his sharp diagnosis of modern *ressentiment*, but should reject the remedy he proposes. Returning to the violence of real vengeance is choosing for the destruction of humankind.[38] Therefore, if humankind wants to survive its own violence, there is only one option: siding with the Crucified One, against Dionysus.

## 3. Evaluation

### a. Girard vs. Vattimo: Violent Transcendence and Transcendence of Love

As we have seen, Vattimo rejects what he designates as an 'apocalyptic and tragic' or 'existentialist' Christianity, in which God is identified as the 'Wholly Other'. Vattimo's own account of Christianity, however, is, as we have pointed out above, also one-sided. While tragic religiosity runs the risk of completely removing God from the world, in this way neglecting the event of the incarnation, in Vattimo's view, transcendence seems to disappear in immanence. In this way, Vattimo is merely offering a Christian legitimization for the abandonment of Christianity. This shows that, though Vattimo appeals to the authority of Girard for his

---

[37] Cf. Vanheeswijck, *Voorbij het onbehagen*, p. 158.
[38] Vanheeswijck, *Voorbij het onbehagen*, p. 158.

position, he is actually only retaining half of the latter's view. Vattimo follows Girard in distinguishing between natural religiosity and Christianity, but ignores his critical stance towards modernity. For modernity is not only the result of the impact of the Gospel message on Western civilization, but also its incomplete realization. The critique of the sacrificial order has not resulted in the Kingdom of God, a Kingdom of universal peace, but in a world dominated by *ressentiment* and global capitalism, a world, moreover, which is threatened by nuclear arms and other weapons of mass destruction. As we have seen above, Vattimo is reducing the narrative particularity of the Bible to a vague and soft message on friendliness. This postmodern Christianity, however, does not seem able to cope with the current situation of *ressentiment*, global capitalism and universal violence.

This, of course, raises the question of whether it is possible to avoid both the Scylla of tragic Christianity and the Charybdis of a Christian legitimization of secularization *à la* Vattimo and Altizer. Is there a way to avoid total immanence without having to return to pre-modern, violent forms of transcendence? For Girard, there is, and this alternative precisely consists in the Christian understanding of 'transcendence-in-immanence'.[39] As Girard points out in *Things Hidden*, his non-sacrificial interpretation of the Gospel message does not result in the erasing of divine transcendence. On the contrary, it enables us to discover the true transcendence beyond the humanly created transcendence of violence. That true transcendence is a transcendence of love. This loving transcendence is 'so far from us, in its very closeness, that we did not even suspect it to be there' (*TH* 217). This transcendence of love is Girard's answer to the question of the uniqueness of Christianity. It is what distinguishes it from natural religiosity with its violent transcendence, but is also the reservation which Christianity makes vis-à-vis modernity. Christianity criticizes modernity insofar as it clings to the old, sacrificial understanding of transcendence and therefore rejects it as by definition violent and oppressive. Because modernity retains the old understanding of transcendence, it believes that humanity can only become truly itself, truly

[39] Vanheeswijck, *Voorbij het onbehagen*, pp. 153–54.

free, by getting rid of transcendence completely. In this regard, postmodernism turns out to be a continuation of this attachment to the view of transcendence as violent. Against the violent transcendence of natural religiosity, Christianity does not oppose the immanentism of modernity, but another kind of transcendence, the transcendence of love, which is even more transcendent than the transcendence of natural religiosity. The latter is humanly created, resulting from our human constitution, while only the former is truly divine.

In this respect, Vattimo's postmodern Christianity also remains tributary to a conception of transcendence as violent. Because he cannot imagine a non-violent transcendence, every form of transcendence has to be secularized. In this regard, it should be noted that Vattimo is caught in the middle between his nihilism (inspired by Nietzsche and Heidegger) and his profession of caritas as the core of the Biblical message. As we have said while discussing Vattimo above, the role of the caritas is to be a kind of categorical imperative, which directs and limits the process of secularization. With the help of the caritas, Vattimo avoids complete relativism. For, after objective reality has disappeared, only a never ending 'battle of interpretations' seems to be left. Caritas is then a criterion on the basis of which one can judge conflicting interpretations and actions. Only those interpretations and actions that are in correspondence with it are valid. The others should be rejected. Caritas can thus be described as a principle that steers the conflict of interpretations in the right direction. In this way, however, it turns out to be something absolute, something transcendent, namely a principle that is valid always and everywhere and, as a consequence, is not bound to time or space. But, as we have pointed out with the help of Jonkers, there is actually no room for such a transcendent principle in Vattimo's nihilistic philosophy. Indeed, as Vattimo is rejecting the belief in objective reality, how can he then still hold an objective principle? Moreover, why should we choose caritas to guide us when we have to decide between conflicting interpretations? Vattimo defends his choice by stating that love is the core of the Biblical message (see above). This, however, cannot be called a real justification. Is he not merely choosing for caritas as principle, because he has already chosen for Christianity? From the perspective of nihilism, the problem is thus not that Vattimo's weak thought is too radical, but that it is not radical enough. Or, phrased differently, his nihilism is not nihilistic enough. He still holds to a principle that is considered as being objective (in the sense that it is considered as not being postulated by the subject). But why would the principle of caritas escape the criticism of Nietzsche? If all reality is posited by the human subject, as nihilism states and Vattimo defends (*B* 30), why would the principle of caritas not also be a construction of the Will to Power? From the perspective of the Biblical message, however, the problem is that Vattimo is too nihilistic, too influenced by Nietzsche and Heidegger, to be able to take the God of the Bible seriously. The Love of which the Bible speaks is not merely a principle, neither a categorical imperative nor a formal commandment, but a Living Presence, a Loving Person.

## b. Does Girard Offer a Christology for a Scientific Age?

In an age of science, the search for the uniqueness of Christianity is of the highest importance because, as we have indicated above, due to the naturalistic critique of religion, we can no longer take the supernatural origin of Christianity for granted. Therefore, in order to defend the possibility of such a superhuman origin of Christianity, we have to attempt to demonstrate the plausibility of such an origin starting from the natural condition of humankind. This precisely accounts for the attractiveness of Girard's Christology, based as it is on a description of the natural condition of humankind in terms of the imitative character of human desire and the victimage mechanism that appears as a way to deal with the violence that follows from the fact that human beings imitate each other's desires. Even more attractive is the fact that Girard's view on the origins of culture can be substantiated with the help of recent insights of the so-called 'hard' sciences. In what follows, we will examine how this can be done.

### b.1. The Turn to Imitation in Natural Science

When Girard developed his theory in the 1960s and 1970s, imitation was, as indicated by Scott Garrels in his 2004 paper

*Imitation, Mirror Neurons & Mimetic Desire: Convergent Support for the Work of René Girard*, definitely out of fashion. It is only after Girard had gained insight into the pivotal role of imitation for the whole of human culture (cf. the phrase from *TH* 7 quoted above), through his study of literature, myths and religious texts, that also the hard sciences in their turn began to appreciate the central place of imitation in the life of the human species.[40] A first important step in this direction was taken in developmental psychology. Until the latter part of the 1970s psychologists accepted Jean Piaget's view that the ability to imitate is only gradually acquired by young children in the course of their first years of life and that it remains in any case a quite inferior and even mindless phenomenon not worth paying much attention to. This changed in 1977 when two psychologists, Andrew Meltzoff and Keith Moore, revolutionized the field of child psychology by publishing a paper in the journal *Science* in which they announced that their attempt to test Piaget's stages of preverbal learning had resulted in the discovery (contra Piaget) that newborns of only a couple of weeks old are already able to imitate facial expressions and manual gestures.[41] At that moment, however, the underlying mechanisms, making imitation possible remained in the dark.

This began to change from 1996 onwards after a research team under the leadership of the Italian neuroscientist Giacomo Rizzolatti discovered the existence of so-called 'mirror neurons' in a particular area of the pre-motor cortex of macaque monkeys known by brain scientists as area F5. These mirror neurons were found by Rizzolatti and his team to become 'active both when the monkey performed a given action and when it observed a similar action performed by the experimenter'. From this, they concluded 'that mirror neurons form a system for matching observation and

---

[40] Scott R. Garrels, 'Imitation, Mirror Neurons & Mimetic Desire: Convergent Support for the Work of René Girard' [paper presented during the 2004 annual conference of the Colloquium on Violence and Religion (COV&R)], p. 29. The paper can be read online at: http://girardianlectionary.net/covr2004/garrelspaper.pdf (access on December 10, 2007).

[41] Cf. Andrew N. Meltzoff and M. Keith Moore, 'Imitation of Facial and Manual Gestures by Human Neonates', *Science* vol. 198 no. 4312 (1977), pp. 74–78.

execution of motor actions'.[42] In this way, the mirror neurons seem to be the neurological foundation of imitation which precisely asks for such a coordination of observation and motor actions. Rizzolatti's team concludes its paper by stating that there are strong reasons to accept that a similar 'mirror system' also exists in humans. They further suggest that – given the fact that the equivalent in the human brain of area F5 in the macaque brain is (or at least includes) Broca's area, the part of the human brain which plays an important role in the production of speech – 'neurons with properties similar to that of monkey "mirror neurons", but coding phonetic gestures, should exist in human Broca's area and should represent the neurophysiological substrate for speech perception'.[43]

The discovery of the mirror neurons inspired the Indian-American neurologist Vilayanur S. Ramachandran in 2000 to the prediction 'that mirror neurons will do for psychology what DNA did for biology: they will provide a unifying framework and help explain a host of mental abilities that have hitherto remained mysterious and inaccessible to experiments'. He expects that mirror neurons will in particular be useful for shedding light on the many mysteries still surrounding the evolution of the human

---

[42] Vittorio Gallese, Luciano Fadiga, Leonardo Fogassi, Giacomo Rizzolatti, 'Action Recognition in the Premotor Cortex', *Brain* 119 (1996), pp. 593–609 (593).

[43] Gallese, Fadiga, Fogassi, Rizzolatti, 'Action recognition', pp. 606–07. Both the existence of a mirror system in the human brain and its role for language have been confirmed by subsequent research. See: Giacomo Rizzolatti and Michael A. Arbib, 'Language within our Grasp', *Trends in Neuroscience* 21/5 (1998) pp. 188–94; Marco Iacoboni, Roger P. Woods, Marcel Brass, Harold Bekkering, John C. Mazziotta, Giacomo Rizzolatti, 'Cortical Mechanisms of Human Imitation', *Science* vol. 286 no. 5449 (1999) pp. 2526–28; Giacomo Rizzolatti, Leonardo Fogassi, Vittorio Gallese, 'Neurophysiological Mechanisms Underlying the Understanding and Imitation of Action', *Nature Reviews: Neuroscience* vol. 2 no. 9 (2001) pp. 661–70; Marc Heiser, Marco Iacoboni, Fumiko Maeda, Jake Marcus, John C. Mazziotta, 'The Essential Role of Broca's Area in Imitation', *European Journal of Neuroscience* 17/5 (2003) pp. 1123–28; Giacomo Rizzolatti and Laila Craighero, 'The Mirror-Neuron System', *Annual Review of Neuroscience* 27 (2004), pp. 169–92; Marco Iacoboni, 'Neural Mechanisms of Imitation', *Current Opinion in Neurobiology* 15 (2005) pp. 632–37.

brain and mind.[44] Whether this will indeed be the case remains to be seen, but in the meantime imitation has also received attention from evolutionary biologists. We turn to this in the next subsection.

### b.2. Big Brained, Imitating Animals

The most marked trend in human evolution is without a doubt a great and rapid expansion of brain size. While the australopithecines appeared on the scene (some 4.5 million years ago) with a brain only slightly bigger than a chimpanzee's and did not experience a significant increase in their brain size during the long period (of 3.5 million years) that they lived on our planet, with the appearance of *Homo* (by 2.5 million years ago) an explosive increase in brain size took off. Over less than 3 million years, the human brain has tripled in size. Australopithecines had a brain size between 400 and 500 cm³; modern humans, on the other hand, reach on average 1350 cm³. Since our bodies did not grow at the same pace, human brains have increasingly become bigger in comparison with the rest of the body. This can also be derived from the 'encephalization quotient' (EQ), which is a measure of brain size in relation to body size. Contemporary chimpanzees have an EQ of 2.0 (which implies that they are already brainier than the average mammal of their size); early australopithecines had an EQ ranging between 2.3 and 2.6; modern humans, however, reach an EQ of 5.8.[45]

All this seems to suggest that accounting for human evolution comes down to accounting for this spectacular increase of the human brain. Indeed, as British psychologist Susan Blackmore argues, our big brains should make us wonder. For, first, the brain is expensive to have. As Blackmore indicates, it continuously uses the amount of energy needed to make a light bulb work. This implies that, when a body is at rest, some 20 per cent of the energy

---

[44] Vilayanur S. Ramachandran, 'Mirror Neurons and Imitation Learning as the Driving Force behind the "Great Leap Forward" in Human Evolution', http://www.edge.org/documents/archive/edge69.html (access on December 10, 2007).

[45] Roger Lewin and Robert A. Foley, *Principles of Human Evolution* (Oxford: Blackwell, 2nd edn, 2004) p. 450.

it uses is consumed by the brain, while the brain is only good for 2 per cent of the body's mass. Second, the brain is also expensive to make. As a result, having big-brained babies requires a lot of energy from the mothers bringing them into the world. Third, having such big-brained babies is not without risk. The brain size of a newborn baby is only about 385 cm$^3$. Though this is less than one-third of the size of an adult brain, it is still twice as large as the brain of a newborn ape of comparable body size. As a result, a human baby's skull, even though it is soft and only hardens towards one year after birth, is simply too big to make an easy birth possible. Moreover, a human baby is born very premature. Most of its brain development only takes place after birth. The brain of a newborn baby even triples in size within a few years. Human babies are thus utterly helpless and defenceless, and remain so for a long time. Thus, they have to rely on parental care for many years, which is something highly exceptional in the animal kingdom. As Roger Lewin and Robert Foley indicate, the necessity of such an extended period of parental care must have had far-reaching consequences for the way hominins had to organize their social life.[46]

When taking into account that the human brain is such an extremely costly organ, the following question immediately pops up: Why did the hominins develop such huge brains? Of course, being more intelligent helps a creature in adapting itself to the challenges of its environment. Human intelligence, however, seems to have developed far beyond the measure necessary for mere survival in a simple foraging context. Or, as Blackmore puts it:

> Not only do we have language but we have invented fridge-freezers, the internal combustion engine and rocket technology; we can (well, some of us can) play chess, tennis and *Mega-Death 6*; we listen to music, dance and sing; and we have created democracy, social security systems and the stock market.[47]

---

[46] Susan Blackmore, *The Meme Machine* (Oxford: Oxford University Press, 2000) pp. 70–71; Lewin and Foley, *Human Evolution*, p. 449.

[47] Blackmore, *The Meme Machine*, p. 67.

Such an excessive development asks for an explanation. For, as Blackmore notes, 'a smaller brain would certainly save a lot of energy, and evolution does not waste energy for no reason'.[48]

Traditionally, answers to the question of why the hominins developed such an enormous brain belong to two main categories. A first group of theories seeks the impetus for human brain development in the challenges posed to the early hominins by their physical environment. This approach has been the most popular one for a long time. According to this view, the early humans became more intelligent in order to deal with the increasingly harder circumstances in a drier, less forested and more seasonal environment with less abundance of food all through the year and with coarser food of lower quality. Researchers defending this view stress the fact that the main difference between apes and humans is that only humans make tools. Friedrich Engels, for instance, also defended this view in *The Part Played by Labour in the Transition of Ape to Man*. In this text, Engels stated that an upright posture freed the hands for the use of tools and this use of tools drove, according to Engels, the growth of the human brain. Thus, in his view, a big brain, intelligence and language are all the products of the fact that humans started to use tools.[49] A strong argument in favour of this view is that the beginning of the massive increase in human brain size coincides with the appearance of the first stone tools some 2.5 million years ago. The question remains, however, whether the use of tools does not already require a large brain instead of being its main cause. Indeed, making even the simplest stone tool requires the planning of a procedure to follow and a considerable amount of insight in the material used. These requirements seem to ask for intelligence already greater than that found in the average ape.[50]

A second group of theories, in contrast, finds the main cause of the growth of the human brain in an increasingly demanding social life. More recently, this second approach has become the most popular explanation for the increase of the human brain.

[48] Blackmore, *The Meme Machine*, p. 70.
[49] As mentioned in Alan Woods and Ted Grant, *Reason in Revolt: Marxist Philosophy and Modern Science* (Marxism in the New Millennium, 1; London: Wellred Publications, 1995) p. 227.

Researchers adopting this view, take as their starting point the paradox that, while apes are noticeably brainier than the average mammal of their size (a chimpanzee, for instance, having, as we have already seen above, an EQ of 2.0), their practical daily life is, since they are living in areas in which there is plenty of food through the year, not so demanding and even quite simple. As a result, one can wonder why the apes nevertheless need the amount of intelligence they have. Moreover, monkeys are less brainy than the apes and they nonetheless succeeded in adapting to circumstances which are far less friendly than the tropical rainforests in which the surviving great apes withdrew. This seems to minimize the importance of the impact of challenging circumstances in becoming brainier, at least in the case of the still surviving great apes. But what then caused the intelligence of the great apes? Primatologists have discovered that, while the life of the great apes is indeed quite simple in the realm of subsistence, their social life is highly complex. As Lewin and Foley point out, apes are constantly busy observing others, trying to outdo them, looking for alliances, creating bonds of friendship and plotting

---

[50] As also admitted by Woods and Grant, who write:

> To work efficiently, the stone knapper has to choose a rock of the correct shape, bearing the correct angle at which to strike; and the striking motion itself requires great practice in order to deliver the appropriate amount of force in the right place. 'It seems clear that early tool-making proto-humans had a good intuitive sense of the fundamentals of working stone,' [Nicholas] Toth [who spent many years attempting to reconstruct the methods by which early humans produced tools] wrote in a paper in 1985. 'There's no question that the earliest toolmakers possessed a mental capacity beyond that of apes,' he recently told me. 'Toolmaking requires a coordination of significant motor and cognitive skills' (*Reason in Revolt*, p. 269 [quoted from Richard Leakey, *The Origin of Mankind*, Science Master Series (New York, NY: Basic Books, 1996) p. 38]; see also *Reason in Revolt*, pp. 278–80).

Yet Woods and Grant seem unaware of the fact that the fragment they quote precisely puts into question their strong claim that the increase in human brain size was fuelled by the making of tools. Since, making tools already requires 'a mental capacity beyond that of apes', where did that mental capacity come from in the first place?

together.[51] According to the second approach, it was this need to be ever more sly and crafty in social matters that drove the growth of the human brain. However, also this explanation is not without difficulties. Exactly as does the use of tools, a complex social life including plotting and scheming in order to outdo rivals also seems rather to presuppose intelligence and a big brain instead of accounting for it. Moreover, something must have changed around 2.5 million years ago in order that one primate species, namely the *Homo*-lineage, started to grow such huge brains, while australopithecines functioned adequately with their smaller brain all during the long period of 3.5 million years in which they lived on our planet, and the great apes probably did not even have a significant increase in brain size since the time the common ancestors of apes and humans strolled around in the tropical rainforests some 6 million years ago.

So, when in search of an explanation for the significant increase in human brain size, we have to take into account that around 2.5 million years ago when their massive increase in brain size began the hominins were already, as were their cousins the great apes, significantly brainier than most other mammals. And mammals, in turn, are also already brainier than earlier classes of animals. We may thus safely state that becoming brainier is a general trend in the evolution of life on earth. This is certainly not to claim that braininess necessarily had to occur. Claiming so would be reintroducing a kind of teleology that Darwin's theory of evolution dispelled from thinking about nature. Evolution is a blind process and does not proceed according to a pre-established plan. Yet, once evolution 'discovers' braininess, a trend to ever more braininess becomes unavoidable. When within a species some mutation creates a distinction between brainier and less brainy individuals, the brainier ones will be able to deal with the challenges of life in a more satisfactory way. As a result, more of the brainier individuals will survive to reproduce themselves and pass on their genes to the next generation, including those genes responsible for their being brainier. In this way, the genes resulting in less brainy individuals will be gradually eliminated from the gene pole of the species through competition.

[51] Lewin and Foley, *Human Evolution*, p. 456.

While the trend towards ever more braininess is in principle without limit, in practice a species will not be able to grow an ever larger brain. As long as a still larger brain results in survival advantage, the brains of a species will indeed become bigger. Yet, once a certain brain size has been reached, developing a still larger brain will no longer result in a significant increase in survival advantage and the disadvantages of a large brain (for instance, as we have already seen, its being costly to make and have, its being responsible for more difficult birth and a longer period of child dependency) will begin to outweigh the possible survival advantage. So, when a certain brain size has been reached, it becomes a disadvantage to develop a still larger brain. Moreover, there are also anatomical restrictions on the possible brain size a species may have. A body simply cannot support a brain that is too big. As a result, we may expect that, once a certain brain size has been reached, the increase in brain size will level off and eventually come to a stop. This may be the reason why the brain size of both australopithecines and the currently living great apes did not grow significantly during such a long period.

The fact that, after a long period of stagnation during the time of the australopithecines, around 2.5 million years ago a spurt of massive increase in brain size could take off demonstrates that at that moment something must have happened; something making it possible that the disadvantages of a bigger brain were again outweighed by its survival advantage or something by which certain anatomical restrictions were overcome and which enabled the Homo-lineage to develop a brain that would finally triple in size in comparison with other great apes and earlier hominins. To date, scientists do not agree on what event made it possible that Homo developed brains far beyond the limits that still seemed to restrict the australopithecines and still seem to restrict the currently living great apes. American anthropologist Dean Falk, for instance, has suggested that a further increase in brain size only became possible after a better distribution of blood vessels in the brain had come into being, enabling efficient cooling of this heat-sensitive organ (a theory known as 'the radiator hypothesis').[52] According to this

[52] Lewin and Foley, *Human Evolution*, p. 451.

view, the australopithecines simply could not develop bigger brains because they lacked this cooling system. The trend towards more braininess was thus blocked by the fact that with australopithecine anatomy a bigger brain would simply overheat.

Another explanation for the big brain of humans is offered by Blackmore in her *The Meme Machine*, in which she defends the thesis that what makes humans unique in the animal kingdom is their ability to imitate. She defines imitation as 'learning to do an act from seeing it done', or to put it differently, 'in imitation a new behaviour is learned by copying from someone else'.[53] In this regard, it is important to distinguish true imitation from both contagion and social learning. (1) We can speak about *contagion* when a particular behaviour stimulates the same behaviour in another individual. For instance, when one animal utters an alarm call and the others of his group respond by repeating it. Contagion is also found among humans. When, for instance, everyone around you is laughing, it is very difficult not start laughing also. The same applies for yawning and coughing, but also for moods and emotions. This, however, is, according to Blackmore, not true imitation because we do not learn something new, but are stimulated to do something we already able to do.[54] (2) In the case of *social learning* the example of one individual stimulates another to do the same. What is learned, however, is not a new kind of behaviour, but only a new application of a behaviour already known. Blackmore gives the example of tits beginning to peck milk bottles in the early 1920s in England. This looks like true imitation, but it is not. Actually, each bird has to reinvent the milk bottle pecking again itself. The example of one bird only leads a second one in a situation in which it is likely to discover in its turn that pecking milk bottles results in access to cream.[55] The same process may also account for the phenomenon of so-called 'chimpanzee cultures', the fact that, as mentioned by Lewin and Foley, 'different communities of chimpanzee display

---

[53] Blackmore, *The Meme Machine*, p. 47.
[54] Blackmore, *The Meme Machine*, p. 47.
[55] Blackmore, *The Meme Machine*, pp. 47–48 and pp. 49–50.

their own particular patterns of behaviour giving rise to the idea that each has its unique cultural traditions'.[56]

True imitation, in contrast, is rare in the animal kingdom. With the exception of humans, it is only found on a regular basis in birdsong.[57] Chimpanzees and gorillas can imitate, but do so only when stimulated by humans and not in the wild. Furthermore, only for humans has imitation become something that is always and spontaneously done. As Blackmore notes:

> Human infants are able to imitate a wide range of vocal
> sounds, body postures, actions on objects and even com-
> pletely arbitrary actions like bending down to touch your
> head on a plastic panel. . . . Unlike any other animals, we
> readily imitate almost everything and anything, and seem
> to take pleasure in doing so.[58]

It has already been stated that becoming brainier (or more intelligent) is a general trend in the evolution of life on earth. This trend can also be understood as 'the building of more and more sophisticated "reality" in a species' head'[59] and as an increasing capacity to learn. When a species acquires the trick of imitation, this capacity takes a huge step forwards. For, from that moment on, it is no longer needed that each individual reinvents the wheel. As we have seen, without imitation the furthest an organism can get is to be brought, by another organism, into a situation in which it is likely to discover the new (application of a) behaviour itself. This absence of true imitation explains the lack of development in the so-called chimpanzee cultures just mentioned above. A chimpanzee young, for instance, does not copy its mother's behaviour, but has to repeat the hard work of trial and error for itself. As a result, there is among chimpanzees no quick accumulation of learned insights and skills as can be found in human cultures, which are based on imitation and in

---

[56] Lewin and Foley, *Human Evolution*, p. 461.
[57] Blackmore even gives the example of blackbirds singing like an alarm clock or imitating a car alarm (Blackmore, *The Meme Machine*, p. 49).
[58] Blackmore, *The Meme Machine*, p. 50.
[59] Lewin and Foley, *Human Evolution*, p. 448.

which a new generation constantly builds upon the results of the work of the previous generation.

Imitation provides us with a possible answer to the question of what happened 2.5 million years ago that made it possible for the *Homo*-lineage to develop such an enormous brain. Since imitation is what seems to distinguish humans from the other animals, we may put forward the hypothesis that what happened at that moment, was that, by some genetic change, some hominins acquired the ability to imitate. Being able to imitate provides an individual with a huge survival advantage. For, when somebody else has, by trial and error, bumped into some useful trick, you can also acquire it without having to go through a long and difficult period of trial and error yourself.[60] As a result, from the moment imitation is discovered, a 'selection for imitation' comes into being. When, by some genetic difference, some hominins were able to imitate, while others were not, the imitators led a better life than those not being able to imitate. They could, for instance, acquire stone tool technology and got, as a result, better food. Consequently, they were healthier, lived longer and produced more and healthier offspring, offspring which was also able to imitate. This importance of imitation called into being an environment in which having better imitation skills provided with a significant survival advantage. As a result, from then on, any genetic characteristic enhancing imitation skills would spread in the gene pole of the species and in this way a trend towards ever better imitation skills came into being.[61]

According to Blackmore, this trend towards better imitation skills can account for the big brain of the *Homo*-lineage, if we make another assumption, namely that being a good imitator requires being a highly intelligent creature and thus having a big brain.[62] That is why *the ability to imitate could only appear in a creature that was already quite brainy*. For, 'imitation requires three skills: making decisions about what to imitate, complex transformations from one point of view to another, and the production of

[60] Blackmore, *The Meme Machine*, p. 75.
[61] Blackmore, *The Meme Machine*, p. 77.
[62] Blackmore, *The Meme Machine*, p. 80.

matching bodily actions'.[63] As Blackmore states, since these skills are nowadays found in many primate species, we may suppose they were also shared by our ancestors of 5 million years ago.[64] *Yet, since becoming a better imitator implies survival advantage, once a species crosses the threshold of imitation,* as we have just mentioned above, *a selective pressure comes into being for becoming a better imitator and thus,* since more intelligence implies better imitation skills, *for more intelligence, for a bigger brain.* So, once our hominin ancestors had acquired the trick of imitation, the equilibrium between the trend to grow a bigger brain and its disadvantages, in the australo-pithecines found in a brain of about 450 cm$^3$, became unbalanced: in the new situation that arose after the introduction of imitation, the risks of the possible disadvantages of a bigger brain were, from now on, again outweighed by the fact that growing such a brain would enable one to become a better imitator and in this way obtain a considerable survival advantage.[65]

### b.3. From Imitation to Memetics

In *The Meme Machine* Blackmore also takes a further step. She not only defends the thesis that what makes humans unique in the animal kingdom is our ability to imitate, she also presents a Darwinian view of culture. In order to elaborate on this, we should first go back to the 1976 bestselling book *The Selfish Gene.* In this book Oxford biologist Richard Dawkins defends the view that the unit of natural selection is not the individual nor the species,

---

[63] Blackmore, *The Meme Machine,* p. 75.

[64] Blackmore, *The Meme Machine,* pp. 75–76.

[65] This is not to deny, however, that no other factors played a role in this further increase in brain size. Especially an additional anatomic change making a further increase in brain size possible, as suggested by Falk (see above), cannot be ruled out. Maybe the trick of imitation had already been acquired some time before 2.5 mya, but could only begin to drive a further increase in brain size after some anatomical restriction had been lifted. Moreover, imitation not only makes a bigger brain necessary, it also makes it possible. Acquiring stone tool technology asks for the skill of imitation, but, once acquired, it also enables an easier access to meat, which is a source of the energy-rich fats enabling a further increase in brain size – which is, as we have already seen, a very costly process – and thus also in imitation skills.

but the gene.[66] Or, as Blackmore puts it, 'evolution is best under-stood in terms of the competition between genes'.[67] Taking the gene as the basic unit of evolution implies a complete reversal of the traditional perspective. In stead of the genes being an instrument used by individuals (or by the species) to reproduce themselves, individuals are now considered as the instruments (Dawkins speaks about 'vehicles', 'survival machines' and 'engines of self-preservation') in the service of the replication of the genes.

In what way can we make sense of Dawkins's (and Blackmore's) claim that evolution is all about competition between the units of hereditary information which Dawkins designates as 'genes'? We can appreciate their view when we take into account that life, as mentioned by Dawkins, began when in the primeval soup the first replicator came into being; or to put it differently: when a simple molecule started to make copies of itself.[68] The closest analogy to these first living organisms in the contemporary world is probably the viruses. A virus is nothing but a piece of heredi-tary material (nucleic acid; RNA or DNA) wrapped in a thin coat of protein. This analogy, though it may give us an impression of the character of the first replicators, does not hold fully. For, as distinct from the first replicators in the primeval soup, contempo-rary viruses are parasitic; they have to infect the cells of a host in order to reproduce themselves. Yet, the analogy is still useful because, like contemporary viruses, the first replicators were nothing but pieces of hereditary material making copies of them-selves. Thus, the wide variety of living organisms on our planet all evolved from these simple replicating molecules. But how did this happen?

Sometimes, a copy slightly differed from its original. In this way, the basis for the evolution of all life on earth was already established. For, ultimately, evolution only needs the fulfilment of three basic conditions in order to begin: (1) there is at least one replicator, something that makes copies of itself (the condition of

---

[66] See note 8 for the complete reference.
[67] Blackmore, *The Meme Machine*, p. 4.
[68] Dawkins, *The Selfish Gene*, pp. 14–16.

R

heredity), (2) not all copies made are identical (the condition of variation) and (3) these differences have an impact, be it negative or positive, on survival advantage in an environment that can only support a limited number of copies (the condition of selection). Consequently, copies sharing some characteristic that has a positive impact on survival advantage will be favoured. They will exist longer and produce themselves more copies; in this way spreading the characteristic that gives them this advantage through the population.[69] In this situation, evolution necessarily has to occur. Blackmore puts this as follows:

> If there is a replicator that makes imperfect copies of itself only some of which survive, then evolution simply *must* occur. This *inevitability* of evolution is part of what makes Darwin's insight so clever. All you need is the right starting conditions and evolution just has to happen.[70]

To put it differently, evolution is an algorithm, 'a mindless procedure which, when followed, must produce an outcome'. Blackmore concludes that:

> If a system is set up so that it follows a given procedure then it does not also need a little mind, or extra-something, inside to make it work. It just must mindlessly happen. This is why [the American philosopher Daniel] Dennett describes Darwin's theory as 'a scheme for creating Design out of Chaos without the aid of Mind'. The design simply must come about when millions of creatures, over millions of years, produce more offspring than can survive.[71]

In the final chapter of his *The Selfish Gene*, Dawkins speculates on the existence of other kinds of replicators, next to the genes,

---

[69] For a more extensive discussion of this, I refer to: Dawkins, *The Selfish Gene*, pp. 16–19.
[70] Blackmore, *The Meme Machine*, pp. 10–11.
[71] Blackmore, *The Meme Machine*, pp. 11–12. Blackmore is referring here to Daniel C. Dennet, *Darwin's Dangerous Idea: Evolution and the Meanings of Life* (London: The Penguin Press, 1995) p. 50.

77

that can be the units of their own evolutionary process. Blackmore adopts this suggestion of Dawkins by stressing that 'replicator' should be considered as a general term. Genes are one kind of replicator, namely the one that drove the evolution of life on earth. But other replicators may be possible. For, as Blackmore – following Dennett – states, the algorithm of evolution can run on any system that fulfils the three basic conditions of evolution mentioned above: heredity (or retention), variation, and selection (an idea Blackmore designates as 'Universal Darwinism').[72]

But does another kind of replicator really exist? In *The Selfish Gene*, Dawkins states that this is indeed the case. In it, he speaks about 'the meme', a word coined in analogy to 'the gene', as such a new replicator.[73] Dawkins gives the following examples of memes: tunes, ideas, catch-phrases, clothes fashions, ways of building pots or of building arches; but also belief in a God and an afterlife, fashions in diet, ceremonies, customs and technologies.[74] Blackmore's *The Meme Machine* attempts to develop the suggestions from the final chapter of *The Selfish Gene*. As she points out, from the moment imitation is 'discovered' by natural selection, another evolutionary system comes into being. Its basic unit is no longer a replicating molecule, but another replicator, 'the meme'. In the course of *The Meme Machine*, Blackmore offers a number of definitions of this new replicator. The meme is 'the something which is passed on when you imitate someone else', 'a unit of imitation', 'everything you have learned by imitation from someone else', an instruction 'for carrying out behaviour, stored in brains (or other objects) and passed on by imitation', and 'whatever it is that is passed on by imitation'.[75] As we have mentioned the viruses as the prototypical replicators in the realm of biology, Blackmore now refers to computer viruses as the prototypical

---

[72] Blackmore, *The Meme Machine*, p. 11.
[73] Dawkins, *The Selfish Gene*, p. 192: 'We need a name for the new replicator, a noun that conveys the idea of a unit of cultural transmission, or a unit of *imitation*. "Mimeme" comes from a suitable Greek root, but I want a monosyllable that sounds a bit like "gene". I hope my classicist friends will forgive me if I abbreviate mimeme to *meme*.'
[74] Dawkins, *The Selfish Gene*, p. 192.
[75] Blackmore, *The Meme Machine*, p. 4, p. 6, p. 17 and p. 43 respectively.

meme. Indeed, exactly as biological viruses, computer viruses are nothing but pieces of code replicating themselves.[76]

But can memes really count as the unit of a new kind of evolution? As we have seen above, three basic conditions must be fulfilled in order for the evolutionary algorithm to begin, namely the conditions of (1) hereditary (or retention), (2) variation and (3) selection. According to Blackmore, memes do indeed fulfil these three conditions:

> [1] When memes are passed on there is *retention* of some of the ideas or behaviours in that meme – something of the original meme must be retained for us to call it imitation or copying or learning by example.
> [2] Memes certainly come with *variation* – stories are rarely told exactly the same way twice, no two buildings are absolutely identical, and every conversation is unique – and when memes are passed on, the copying is not always perfect.
> [3] There is memetic *selection* – some memes grab the attention, are faithfully remembered and passed on to other people, while others fail to get copied at all.[77]

This shows that memes indeed fulfil the three basic conditions of evolution and that, as a result, once the first meme appeared – at the moment natural selection had created a creature intelligent enough to be able to imitate – the evolutionary algorithm simply took over and called into being an increasingly rich variety of cultural phenomena; precisely as it created the wide variety of living organisms from the moment the first replicator appeared in the primeval soup.

The 'meme's eye view' is, according to Blackmore, a very powerful tool of analysis. Memetics has, she defends, a high explanatory value. It is able to explain why the *Homo*-lineage developed such enormous brain, but it is also useful in illuminating the origin of language,[78] in clarifying why all kinds of strange beliefs – such as the belief in alien abduction, in life after death, in divination

---

[76] Blackmore, *The Meme Machine*, p. 21.
[77] Blackmore, *The Meme Machine*, p. 14.
[78] See for this: Blackmore, *The Meme Machine*, pp. 82–107.

and fortune telling, and in an invisible being called God – can contaminate entire populations,[79] and in explaining why humans are able to be altruistic, generous and cooperative in a way unknown among other animals.[80] Moreover, memetics is able to account for the difference between humans and other animals, without having to fall back on 'mysterious' and 'magical' entities such as a soul or some special spiritual essence. Simultaneously, it enables us to stress the link between humans and the other animals, without falling prey to the narrow reductionism of sociobiology.[81] Memetics also offers an explanation for the transition from nature to culture. Culture simply had to emerge once natural selection brought forth a creature intelligent enough to imitate. In this way, memetic theory overcomes the impasse between biological reductionism and spiritualism indicated above. On the one hand, following the most important lesson of Darwin's theory of evolution, it firmly places humans among the other animals as one of the many products of a process of natural selection; a process which, as we have already seen, 'does not also need a little mind, or extra-something, inside to make it work'.[82] The human brain is as much the outcome of this mind-less process as all the other parts of the human body and the bodies of all the other animals. On the other hand, however, memetics is also able to account for the special place humans occupy within the animal kingdom. Our capacity to imitate is what makes us unique. Though some song birds may, as has been indicated above, be able to imitate sounds and some great apes can indeed be forced to imitate (but only by us humans), no other animal is able to imitate to the extent we are. It is imitation which lies at the basis of the whole of human culture.

### b.4. Memetics or Mimetics?

However, it is still a subject of contention, even among defenders of a Darwinian view of culture, whether it is really necessary to

---

[79] See for this: Blackmore, The Meme Machine, pp. 175–203.
[80] See for this: Blackmore, The Meme Machine, pp. 154–58.
[81] Blackmore, The Meme Machine, p. 154.
[82] See note 74 above.

postulate something as vague as 'memes' to explain human culture. Does memetics tell us something that we not already know? It is indeed remarkable that we were able to offer a Darwinian account of the emergence of human culture without the meme-concept. In this regard, Matthew Taylor has raised the suspicion that the whole idea of memes is nothing but 'a banal truism given a glamorous aura by the language of genetics and computer programming' which does nothing to enhance our understanding of human culture. Taylor even suspects that memetics is an attempt of certain neo-Darwinists, not to explain culture, but 'rather to *explain it away*, perhaps even to formally *exclude* it'. The memes are then the true actors, while human beings are merely the hosts they use to propagate themselves.[83] In this regard, we can refer to Dennett's famous quote in *Darwin's Dangerous Idea* that 'a scholar is just a library's way of making another library'.[84] But, as Taylor rightly notes, 'This seems to imply an extraordinary denial of human agency'.[85] It may not come as a surprise then that Blackmore's *The Meme Machine* concludes with the rejecting of a choosing 'I' as an unnecessary fiction: 'I' am only an illusion, 'a fluid and ever-changing group of memes installed in a complicated meme machine',[86] 'a bunch of memes', 'a vast memeplex', 'the most insidious and pervasive memeplex of all'.[87] Thus, since 'I am nothing but a temporary conglomeration of genes, phenotype, memes, and memeplexes', there is no choosing 'I'. Or, as Blackmore puts it, 'the choices will all be a product of my genetic and memetic history in a given environment, not of some separate self that can "have" a life purpose and overrule the memes that make it up'.[88] In this way, Blackmore's memetics seems to result in a plea for complete determinism: 'free will' is an illusion

[83] Matthew Taylor, 'From Memetics to Mimetics: Richard Dawkins, René Girard, and Media-Related Pathologies' [paper presented during the 2002 annual conference of the Colloquium on Violence and Religion (COV&R)], p. 3. Unfortunately, this paper is no longer available online. I want to thank Geert Van Coillie for providing me with a copy.

[84] Dennett, *Darwin's Dangerous Idea*, p. 346.

[85] Taylor, 'From Memetics to Mimetics', p. 4.

[86] Blackmore, *The Meme Machine*, pp. 241–42.

[87] Blackmore, *The Meme Machine*, p. 231.

[88] Blackmore, *The Meme Machine*, p. 242.

and everything is determined by a complex interplay of genes, memes and environment. This, of course, raises the question of whether it is not – especially in an era in which, as Girard notes, real vengeance is back among us (see above) and in which, one may add, ecological disaster is imminent – dangerous and completely irresponsible to deny human agency in the way Blackmore does.[89]

As has become clear natural science has recently substantiated the pivotal role of imitation for human culture which Girard had already discovered by the time he published *Deceit, Desire, and the Novel* in 1961. At the same time, however, Girard's work enables us to detect the one-sidedness of the way natural scientists treat imitation. Blackmore is an exemplary case in this regard. Though she states, as we have seen above, that human beings always and spontaneously imitate almost everything and anything, she does not draw from this the conclusion that imitation is not only a beneficial thing. If we imitate everything, we also imitate each other's desires and this is the source of rivalry and violence. Blackmore remains blind for this aspect of imitation. The same is the case for Dawkins himself, who is for this reason criticized by Girard in the latter's *Les origines de la culture* (The origins of culture).[90] Moreover, as pointed out by Taylor, it is remarkable 'that Girard, an influential Christian thinker, has put forward an unflinchingly brutal evolutionary scenario as well as a profound demystification of religion' while militant atheists such as Dawkins and Blackmore are content with a rather simplistic rejection of religion as a harmful 'memeplex', a parasite or 'virus of the mind'.[91] This brings Taylor even to the following conclusion:

[89] This raises complex issues which cannot be dealt with here such as the problem of determinism and free will as well as the one of science and ideology. I hope to be able to deal with the ideological sides of memetics in another publication.

[90] René Girard, *Les origines de la culture: Entretiens avec Pierpaolo Antonello et Joao Cezar de Castro Rocha* (Paris: Desclée de Brouwer, 2004) p. 97 and p. 148. Translated into English as: *Evolution and Conversion: Dialogues on the Origins of Culture* (with Joao Cezar de Castro Rocha and Pierpaolo Antonello; London and New York, NY: T&T Clark, 2008) p. 77 and p. 100.

[91] Richard Dawkins, 'Viruses of the Mind', *A Devil's Chaplain: Selected Writings* (London: Weidenfeld & Nicolson, 2003) pp. 128–45 (= section 3.2).

Rather than being demystifying, such an approach [the one of memetics] may itself amount to a kind of ritual expulsion. The memeticians add yet another layer of myth over religion and human nature, leaving us as blind as ever to the way they profoundly structure one another, even when (perhaps especially when) we are trying very hard not to be religious.[92]

Or, as Girard himself had already put it in *Things Hidden*: 'To expel religion is, as always, a religious gesture' (*TH* 32).

## b.5. Conclusion

As we have indicated above, the search for the uniqueness of Christianity is of the highest importance in an age of science because, due to the naturalistic critique of religion, we can no longer take the supernatural origin of Christianity for granted. Therefore, in order to defend the possibility of such a superhuman origin of Christianity, we have to attempt to demonstrate the plausibility of such an origin starting from the natural condition of humankind. The attractiveness of Girard's work is that it precisely offers such a Christology for a scientific age, which receives convergent support from recent insights in developmental psychology, neurobiology and evolutionary theory, but also offers a critique of certain developments within natural science. What Girard teaches us, is that the naturalistic critique of religion forwarded by modern natural science does not necessarily entail the end of Christianity. Proceeding from the natural constitution of humankind (as we learn from science), we have indicated that it is *likely* that Christianity cannot be reduced to just another form of natural religiosity. This brings us at the threshold of Christian faith. For, if Christianity can indeed not be reduced to/deduced from our natural condition, it has to be of supernatural origin. As a result, revelation no longer has to be unintelligible, no longer an insult for natural reason which cannot accept the claims of Christianity merely on authority. If it is not unlikely that Christianity

---

[92] Taylor, 'From Memetics to Mimetics', p. 16.

has a transcendent origin, reason is justified in reaching beyond itself towards a Word which comes from elsewhere.

## c. John Milbank's Critique of Girard

Girard's Christology has not remained without critics. In his magnum opus, *Theology and Social Theory*, John Milbank, one of the major proponents of the Radical Orthodoxy movement, offers a critique of Girard.[93] In the last subsection of our chapter on Girard we will deal with Milbank's criticisms. Milbank raises two major objections against Girard. First, he reproaches the latter of firmly remaining within the positivist tradition of explaining religion in social terms. More in particular, Milbank rejects Girard's view of desire. By stressing the role of the model, so Milbank claims, Girard ignores the possibility of objective desire, i.e. the desire of things which are intrinsically desirable *for themselves*, and in so doing he gives in to the modern, liberal view of the arbitrariness of all desire, which is therefore privileged in Girard's entire attempt to explain religion. In this regard, Milbank also refers to Augustine, who criticized the pagan myths for legitimizing the current legal order by referring to a pre-exist chaos which was *ontologically* prior. According to Milbank, Girard is doing the same by positing a pre-religious phase of rivalry and violence which was subsequently overcome by the installation of the sacrificial order. Augustine, in contrast, has taught us, Milbank adds, that such a phase of anarchy may *historically* have been the case, but that in no way should it be thought as *ontologically necessary*.[94] This criticism is adopted by Hans Boersma, who in his *Violence, Hospitality, and the Cross* objects against Girard that he is not able to think creation as good. For him, Boersma claims, 'violence is so pervasive as to lie at the heart of the created order or of human culture'. Girard seems to identify culture and violence to

---

[93] John Milbank, *Theology and Social Theory: Beyond Secular Reason* (Signposts in Theology; repr., Oxford: Blackwell, 1994) pp. 392–98.

[94] Milbank, *Theology and Social Theory*, p. 394.

such a degree, Boersma adds, that a non-violent culture is simply a *contradictio in terminis*.[95]

This leads us immediately to Milbank's second objection against Girard. Precisely by identifying culture with violence, and in this way leaving no room for a possible non-violent culture, Girard reduces, in Milbank's view, the Christ-event to a merely negative gesture of rejection of existent culture, but without the promotion of an alternative, peaceful practice. It is correct, Milbank states, to stress Jesus' refusal of violence, but one should also take into account the 'concrete "form"' of the latter's non-violence. Again opposing Girard and Augustine, Milbank concludes that we get in the former's work not 'a theology of two cities [as in Augustine], but instead [the] story of one city, and its final rejection by a unique individual'. As a result, Milbank concludes, Girard's work 'cannot really be used to promote an alternative practice taking a collective, political form'.[96] Or, as Boersma puts it, 'Girard's atonement theory cannot translate into a robust political theology'.[97]

To elaborate on his second criticism, Milbank suggests that Girard offers an argument not unlike the one offered by St Anselm who, in his *Cur Deus homo*, stated that only God himself, being free from sin, could really and 'fully "suffer" sin' and was able to make the offering needed to undo the consequences of sin. In a similar vein, according to Girard, Christ *has* to be God incarnate because the truth about violence can only be brought to light by someone who is not held captive by violence and such a person cannot be generated by a world completely dominated by violence. The problem with both Anselm and Girard, Milbank states, is that their arguments 'tend to become dangerously "extrinsicist" in character and unrelated to experience and practice'. Or, to put it differently, 'if Jesus suffered perfectly, or if he alone really refused a dominating violence, then how do we *know* this, how does it "come through to us"?' Is Girard, Milbank seems to be asking, not

---

[95] Hans Boersma, *Violence, Hospitality, and the Cross: Reappropriating the Atonement Tradition* (Grand Rapids, MI: Baker Academic, pb. edn, 2006) p. 145.

[96] Milbank, *Theology and Social Theory*, p. 395.

[97] Boersma, *Violence, Hospitality, and the Cross*, p. 143.

turning the incarnation into a supernatural intervention of some kind of *deus ex machina* who passes by to deliver his message of non-violence, but ultimately disappears again without changing our violent situation and remaining a stranger, not one of us?[98] In this way, Milbank further claims, the Kingdom proclaimed by Jesus is something human beings have to realize themselves (by, as we have seen, collectively renouncing revenge) and therefore 'a purely human work'. Yet, if humans can bring about the Kingdom of peace by their own means, as Girard indeed seems to suggest, the question should be raised whether the argument for the supernatural, non-human origin of the Christ-event and the uniqueness of Christianity has not failed. For, in Milbank's view, Jesus' rejection of violence is not sufficient reason to call him divine:

> Given that the Hebrews had already arrived at a 'partial' rejection of sacrifice, why should they not have arrived at a total one, out of entirely human resources, if all that Jesus really seems to offer is a denial of culture, and not the imagination of something beyond culture, which would indeed be humanly problematic?

According to Milbank, the Christ-event can only be atoning if Christ is not merely revealing the violent origins of culture, but also gives us an alternative, enables a new kind of social existence. This, Milbank states, asks for 'an exemplary practice which we can imitate and which can form the context for our lives together, so that we can call ourselves "the body of Christ".' Or, to put it differently, 'Jesus' "divinity" relates to the demonstration of the possibility of non-violence in a particular "pattern" of existence, not to the intrusion of extra-human enabling capacities'. Salvation, to put it differently, entails the restoration of capacities that were

---

[98] A similar question is raised by Boersma: 'Does Christ have nothing to do with the created order and with the development of culture?' And he concludes as follows: 'Girard's anthropology leads to a theology of culture that is deeply troubling in its separation of culture, creation, and violence, on the one hand, and Church, redemption, and hospitality, on the other' (Boersma, *Violence, Hospitality, and the Cross*, pp. 145–46).

original to humankind, but were corrupted as the result of sin. It is not the acquisition of something added from the outside.[99]

How should we react to Milbank's criticisms? (1) First, we should raise the question of whether Girard's view necessarily implies that humankind and creation are intrinsically evil. This is acknowledged by Boersma who refers to the interview with Girard in *The Girard Reader* where the latter rejects the idea that mimetic desire is essentially bad. For this reason, Boersma feels he has to nuance the first criticism of Milbank. In contrast to what Milbank claims, Boersma states, Girard 'does not remain entirely stuck in an exposure of evil and violence as the basis of the human polis'.[100] Fergus Kerr, in defence of Girard, even states that rivalry is a perverse form of mimesis, 'which is in itself the pacific imitation by a child of its parent or by a disciple of a master'. Imitation, Kerr suggests, is not necessarily violent and he concludes by stating that 'Girard denies any necessity to original violence'.[101] Boersma rejects this conclusion and still holds on to his view that, though imitation is not entirely a bad thing for Girard, he nevertheless considers culture to be good only in a later stage because in the beginning there was violence . . .'[102] The point of discussion here is the one of the ontological priority of violence. According to Milbank and Boersma, Girard claims such a priority for violence. From a theological perspective, such a claim is unacceptable because it would entail subscribing ontological priority to sin, which would be an absolute mockery of the goodness of God and creation. Indeed, in which way can we still speak about a loving Creator if human culture as a whole is always founded on violence? (2) This brings us back to the second criticism of Milbank, namely that Girard's Jesus only rejects existent culture as violent but does not offer an alternative. Against this, it should be noted, as Kerr does, that it is not clear whether Milbank does much better on this point and the question should even be raised whether the development of 'a substantial picture of what

[99] Milbank, *Theology and Social Theory*, pp. 395–97.
[100] Boersma, *Violence, Hospitality, and the Cross*, p. 144.
[101] Fergus Kerr, 'Rescuing Girard's Argument?', *Modern Theology* 8/4 (1992), pp. 385–99 (395 and 397).
[102] Boersma, *Violence, Hospitality, and the Cross*, p. 145.

non-violent practice would be like' is possible at all. Or, as Kerr puts it, 'is it likely, given the pervasiveness of institutionalised violence, that any vision of the alternative can be delineated in much more than negatives and promises?' Moreover, Girard does more than merely reducing the Christ-event to a negative gesture of refusal. As also noted by Boersma, Girard does not reject mimesis *in toto*, but speaks about the imitation of Jesus and, through him, of the Father. In Mt. 5.48, for instance, Jesus calls upon his listeners to 'Be perfect, therefore, as your heavenly Father is perfect'. In the words and deeds of Jesus, something of what a non-violent practice could be begins to shine forth. This is, as Kerr notes, not 'the absolute Christian vision of ontological peace' which Milbank is asking, but that is without a doubt asking too much. This also enables us to meet the first criticism of Milbank. If in Jesus' life and proclamation, a first impression is given of what a non-violent existence could be, Girard's Jesus is precisely doing what Milbank expects from him, namely demonstrating that our captivity by violence is not 'the ultimate cultural "condition" of our being', but that, as Kerr puts it, 'there is a "better" way: a way of life based not on the victimization of others but one where we choose to bear one another's burdens'. And this, Kerr concludes, brings Girard actually very close to Milbank's Augustine. For both, it may have been the case that *historically* speaking violence/anarchy was first, but neither Girard nor Augustine ascribe any necessity or ontological priority to that state of anarchy and violence.[103]

From his criticisms of Girard it also becomes clear that Milbank rejects the idea of a Christology for a scientific age. (1) He explicitly states that we 'must refuse to give a scientific, explanatory account of the sacrificial character of most human cultures'. In this regard, he refers to Wittgenstein who called the fact that most human cultures share sacrificial language something which 'must simply be accepted as a surd coincidence'. The only discipline which can shed some light on this state of affairs, Milbank adds, is theology, which understands it in terms of original sin. This, however, does not mean that theology is able to explain the predominance of sacrificial language because it is not possible to

---

[103] Kerr, 'Rescuing Girard's Argument?', pp. 395–97.

explain sin. (2) We should also refuse, Milbank claims, any attempt to 'test' Jesus' analysis of human culture with the help of science. First of all, that is not possible, because there is no ultimate condition of human culture, but even if it would be possible to formulate such a condition and it would turn out that Jesus did unearth that condition, it would still not follow from it that Jesus is God incarnate.[104]

In defence of the project of a Christology for a scientific age, the following remarks can be made. First, both Milbank's rejection of a scientific investigation of the predominance of sacrificial language as his assumption that there is no such a thing as an ultimate condition of human culture are unjustified. Why is Wittgenstein correct in designating the omnipresence of sacrificial language as nothing but a surd coincidence? Why is an ultimate condition of culture impossible? Refusing to use evidence from science when available seems to result in a Christology which remains locked in its own separated universe of discourse, not able to communicate with a culture which is no longer Christian and which is strongly influenced by the scientific way of thinking. In this way, Milbank threatens to turn Christianity into a counter-culture, which massively rejects the current secular culture as 'bad'. In this regard, the Christology of Girard seems to be much more fruitful because his work enables to appreciate modern, secular culture in a nuanced matter, i.e. without having to accept it uncritically (as Vattimo, as we have seen above, does) or without having to reject it massively (as Milbank does).

Milbank is correct, however, when he states that the possibility that Jesus arrived at a rejection of violence by purely human means cannot be ruled out. This means that the work of Girard, even when it receives convergent support from the natural sciences, is not able to demonstrate in a definitive way the divinity of Christ. It is only able to show that it is *not unlikely* that Christianity cannot be reduced to just another form of natural religiosity and, as I have already said above, this brings us at the threshold of Christian faith and justifies us in reaching beyond ourselves towards a Word which comes from elsewhere.

---

[104] Milbank, *Theology and Social Theory*, p. 395.

Yet, to conclude, it should also be noted that the work of Girard on the uniqueness of Christianity is still in need of further elaboration. In this respect, it is remarkable that the analyses of the Biblical texts in *Things Hidden* appear often less detailed than the text analyses in *Deceit, Desire, and the Novel* or *Violence and the Sacred*. There is also the problem of more or less unfounded ad-hoc hypotheses,[105] which are in need of further substantiation. In this regard, both a verse-by-verse study of the New Testament in light of Girard's theses and a critical evaluation of them in light of the letter of the Biblical texts are necessary if we want to consolidate his view on the uniqueness of Christianity. A similar problem pops up with respect to Girard's interpretation of Nietzsche, which is not based on an extensive study of the latter's oeuvre, but on a discussion of two isolated fragments (namely the fragment from the *Nachlass* on *The Two Types* which we have discussed above

---

[105] For instance: to substantiate his claim that Jesus did not ascribe any violence to God in his parables, Girard has to explain the difference between the way the parable of the murderous tenants of the vineyard ends in Matthew and in Luke. In Matthew, we can read the following: "'Now when the owner of the vineyard comes, what will he do to those tenants?" **They said to him**, "He will put those wretches to a miserable death, and lease the vineyard to other tenants who will give him the produce at the harvest time'" (Mt. 21.40–41), while Luke offers us the following alternative reading: 'What then will the owner of the vineyard do to them? He will come and destroy those tenants and give the vineyard to others' (Lk. 20.15–16). The difference is clear: in Luke, it is Jesus who is ascribing revenge to God, while in Matthew it is only the audience which does this ('they said to him'). For this reason Girard prefers the version of the story as it is found in Matthew and he justifies this choice by postulating that that version is the most original one. The version found in Luke is in his view a later adaptation in which the author of Luke or a later copyist omitted the fact that the violent answer came from Jesus' listeners and not from Jesus himself as an insignificant detail while it is of course, for Girard, the most important element of the text. If we take for granted Girard's presupposition that Jesus did not ascribe any violence to God, this explanation is absolutely justified, but then it can of course no longer be used to substantiate the claim that Jesus did not ascribe any violence to God. To accomplish the latter, one would have to demonstrate the plausibility of the priority of Matthew's version of the parable on other grounds.

and aphorism no. 125 from *The Gay Science*[106]). As we have indicated with the help of Valadier, Girard's interpretation of Nietzsche is not unfounded, but it is nevertheless in need of further substantiation by a more elaborated study of the Dionysian in the work of Nietzsche. The same applies, furthermore, for the intuitions of Girard (and Vanheeswijck) on the relation between Christianity, *ressentiment* and modern capitalism. Though not unlikely, and certainly attractive, these intuitions remain at present largely unfounded. Thus, further study is also necessary in this regard.

---

[106] Aphorism no. 125 of *The Gay Science* is discussed by Girard in 'Dionysus versus the Crucified', 828–35 [255–61]. See also: René Girard, 'The Founding Murder in the Philosophy of Nietzsche', *Violence and Truth: On the Work of René Girard* (ed. Paul Dumouchel; London: The Athlone Press, 1988) pp. 227–46. By interpreting the death of God proclaimed by the madman in aphorism no. 125 in terms of the founding murder, however, Girard seems to be overplaying his hand. Anyway, Girard's interpretation of the death of God in Nietzsche is in need of further study.

# Chapter 3
# Slavoj Žižek

## 1. Introducing Slavoj Žižek

Slavoj Žižek (born in 1949) is a philosopher and Lacanian psychoanalyst. He is currently Professor in the Department of Philosophy of the Faculty of Arts at the University of Ljubljana (Slovenia) and Co-director of the Center for Humanities of Birbeck College (University of London). In 1988 Žižek published his first book outside Slovenia, namely *Le plus sublime des hystériques: Hegel passe*,[1] followed in 1989 by his first book in English with the title *The Sublime Object of Ideology*. In his introduction to this book Žižek states that it has a threefold aim. First, he wants to introduce some fundamental categories of the French psychoanalyst Jacques Lacan. By doing this he wants to contend with two misunderstandings of Lacan. First he wants to make clear that Lacan cannot be aligned with so-called post-structuralism. Second he also wants to dispute the image of Lacan as an obscurantist. Žižek's second and third aims amount to realizing a return to Hegel and contributing to the theory of ideology (in the line of Marx). These three aims are closely connected. According to Žižek, Hegel is not the author of panlogicism, but on the contrary a thinker of contingency and difference. This however can only be demonstrated by reading Hegel with Lacan. This reading of Hegel opens up new possibilities to understand ideology, without falling prey to postmodern temptations like the assertion that we live in a 'post-ideological' era.[2]

---

[1] Slavoj Žižek, *Le plus sublime des hystériques: Hegel passe* (Paris: Point Hors Ligne, 1988).

[2] Slavoj Žižek, *The Sublime Object of Ideology* (Phronesis; London and New York, NY: Verso, 1989) p. 7 (henceforth cited as *SOI*).

# Slavoj Žižek

The thinking of Žižek can thus be considered as having three co-ordinates; namely Hegelian philosophy, Lacanian psychoanalysis and Marxism. Although, one can have serious doubts about the extent to which Žižek deals with these sources in an 'orthodox' manner. In fact, Peter Dews argues that Žižek's Lacanianism is not Hegelian at all.[3] He even wonders if it is Lacanian.[4] Other critics have posited that Žižek's relationship to Marxism is also equivocal.[5] For, Žižek appeared on the international intellectual scene at the moment that Marxism was as good as dead. As the Communist regimes of Eastern Europe crumbled, Western Marxism lost all credibility and support. Yet, *The Sublime Object of Ideology* was published in a series edited by two leading post-Marxists, namely Ernesto Laclau and Chantal Mouffe. Because of this Žižek was also labelled as a post-Marxist. Moreover, in the English-speaking world he became famous thanks to his less political works, in which he introduces Lacan with the help of popular culture. On the basis of these works it seemed justified to consider him as a postmodernist. He was at that time a supporter of the kind of radical democracy which Laclau and Mouffe advocated. This was a further reason to regard him as a post-Marxist. In an interview in 1990 he pleads for a 'postmodern' acceptance of certain limits and the abandonment of utopias.[6] This is exactly what Žižek expressly rejects in more recent work.[7] At the same

[3] See for this: Peter Dews and Peter Osborne, 'Lacan in Slovenia: An Interview with Slavoj Žižek and Renata Salecl', *Radical Philosophy* no. 58 (1991), pp. 25–31 (25–26); Peter Dews, 'Hegel in Analysis: Slavoj Žižek's Lacanian Dialectics', *Bulletin of the Hegel Society of Great Britain* no. 21/22 (1990), pp. 1–18 (1–2). This article has been revised and expanded as 'The Tremor of Reflection: Slavoj Žižek's Lacanian Dialectics', *Radical Philosophy* no. 72 (1995), pp. 17–29.

[4] Dews, 'The Tremor of Reflection', p. 26.

[5] See for this: Sean Homer, 'It's the Political Economy, Stupid! On Žižek's Marxism', *Radical Philosophy* no. 108 (2001), pp. 7–16.

[6] Dews and Osborne, 'Lacan in Slovenia', p. 26: 'For me, it is modernism which insists on the utopian idea of disalienation, while postmodernism is precisely *the recognition that you accept a certain division as the price of freedom*' (emphasis added).

[7] See, for instance, Žižek's contributions in Judith Butler, Ernesto Laclau, and Slavoj Žižek, *Contingency, Hegemony, Universality: Contemporary Dialogues on the Left* (Phronesis; London and New York, NY: Verso, 2000).

time, the question should be asked to what extent Žižek has ever wholeheartedly been a post-Marxist. Already in *The Sublime Object of Ideology* he takes on himself the defence of Althusser, the *bête noire* for post-Marxism and thus a strange move for a so-called post-Marxist. Maybe we should conclude that Žižek never really was a post-Marxist after all and, as a newly emerging 'global intellectual' (Homer), just kept up appearances in a time when post-Marxism was fashionable.

Žižek emerged from a group of Slovenian intellectuals that can be described as 'the Slovenian Lacanian School'. Besides Žižek, Miran Božovič, Mladen Dolar, Renata Salecl (Žižek's former wife) and Alenka Zupančič (among others), are part of this school which came into being in the early 1980s in opposition to the two philosophical tendencies that had dominated the Slovenian academy since the 1970s. The first of these schools, the so-called Praxis School, defended a version of Marxism which ought not to be compared with the orthodox dialectical materialism of the Soviet Union, but was closer to the Western Marxism of Lukács, Gramsci and Adorno. These authors defended a humanist Marxism, based on the earlier writings of Marx (before 1845). The Marxism of the Praxis School was the official philosophy. Beside this, there was also a countermovement of philosophers who oriented themselves mainly on Heidegger and phenomenology. The thinkers of the Slovenian Lacanian School opposed both currents. They criticized the official Marxist ideology, but at the same time they didn't want to fall back on Heidegger.

But why then using Lacan instead? Žižek and his colleagues refer to the peculiar situation in their country to explain this move. In contrast to Western Europe, where Marxism has always remained a countermovement, in Yugoslavia, Western Marxism became the official ideology. According to Žižek and his allies, this resulted in a paradoxical situation. In the Soviet Union under Stalinism the deception was still quite simple: the Party pretended to reign in the name of the People, while everybody knew they reigned out of self-interest. In Yugoslavia the deception was much more ingenious. The official philosophy was a 'Marxism with a human face'. The Party thus pretended to reign in the name of an ideology that precisely stated that the major obstacle for real socialism is the bureaucracy of Party and State. Hence, Slovenian

Slavoj Žižek

intellectuals found in the work of Lacan the instrument to analyse and criticize this situation, without running the risk that their criticism immediately became a part of the system under attack. This was not self-evident, since the system considered itself already as its own worst enemy and already criticized itself.[8]

In his preface to *The Sublime Object of Ideology*, Laclau points out the peculiar character of the Slovenian School within the Lacanian movement. According to Laclau what makes them unique is that they use the work of Lacan explicitly within the frame of a political and philosophical thinking. Their only predecessor in this was Althusser, who considered Lacanian psychoanalysis as offering the only theory of the subject which is in accordance with historical materialism. For, the Slovenian School applies Lacan in a double way: on the one hand, they use him for the critique of ideology, while, on the other hand, they read classical philosophical texts (from Plato, Descartes, Leibniz, Kant, Hegel, Marx, Heidegger) with a Lacanian view (*SOI* x–xi).

Since Žižek's first books were published outside Slovenia at the end of the 1980s, he has kept on publishing in a tearing rush. In her introduction to Žižek's work, Sarah Kay distinguishes three targets at which Žižek aims his criticism.[9] First there is the cluster consisting of post-Marxism, cultural studies, identity politics and multiculturalism. Žižek's criticism of these has become ever more explicit through the years. He basically reproaches their adherents for the fact that in their political battle for more democratic rights and equal treatment of so-called 'minority groups' on the basis of gender, ethnicity, race or sexual inclination they remain blind to the real problem, namely world-wide capitalism. Interestingly, against this he stresses the Marxist orthodoxy, despite the fact that Homer states that his Lacanianism makes it impossible for him to be a real orthodox Marxist.[10] A second target of Žižek's criticism is closely connected with the previous one, namely deconstructionism. Žižek especially targets Jacques Derrida and Judith Butler.

[8] Dews and Osborne, 'Lacan in Slovenia', pp. 25–26; Dews, 'Hegel in Analysis', pp. 1–2.
[9] Sarah Kay, *Žižek: A Critical Introduction* (Key Contemporary Thinkers; Cambridge: Polity, 2003) p. 102.
[10] Homer, 'It's the Political Economy', pp. 14–15.

Christ in Postmodern Philosophy

Finally he clearly resists New Age and so-called neo-paganism, which he labels as spiritualism and neo-Jungian obscurantism.

  Against these different currents of thought Žižek takes on himself the defence of 'the subject' as it has been shaped by modern philosophy. So Žižek begins his 1999 major work *The Ticklish Subject* by stating that his aim is 'to reassert the Cartesian subject', although he immediately adds to this that he is not concerned with 'the guise in which it has dominated modern thought', but with 'its forgotten obverse'.[11] Žižek rejects the postmodern commonplace which states that the transcendental subject is over and done with and that henceforth we may only speak about 'a divided, finite subject, a subject "thrown" into a non-transparent, contingent life-world'. By way of contrast, Žižek 'relies on the full acceptance of the notion of modern subjectivity elaborated by the great German Idealists from Kant to Hegel', which he considers as 'the unsurpassable horizon of our philosophical experience'. The work of Lacan, he adds, is 'a privileged intellectual tool to reactualize German Idealism'.[12]

  Besides a 'return' to Marxist orthodoxy, a second, important evolution can be discerned in the works of Žižek, namely his increasing interest in Christianity which has appeared in such a degree that we can speak about a 'religious turn'. For example, in the last years Žižek published books with titles such as *The Fragile Absolute: Or, Why is the Christian Legacy Worth Fighting For?* (in 2000),[13] *On Belief* (in 2001),[14] and *The Puppet and the Dwarf: The Perverse Core of Christianity* (in 2003).[15] But also in *The Ticklish*

[11] Slavoj Žižek, *The Ticklish Subject: The Absent Centre of Political Ontology* (Wo es war; London and New York, NY: Verso, 1999) p. 2 (henceforth cited as *TS*).

[12] Slavoj Žižek, 'Preface: Burning the Bridges', *The Žižek Reader* (ed. Edmond and Elizabeth Wright; Blackwell Readers; Oxford: Blackwell, 1999) pp. vii–x (ix).

[13] Slavoj Žižek, *The Fragile Absolute: Or, Why is the Christian Legacy Worth Fighting For?* (Wo es war; London and New York, NY: Verso, 2000) (henceforth cited as *FA*).

[14] Slavoj Žižek, *On Belief* (Thinking in Action; London and New York, NY: Routledge, 2001) (henceforth cited as *OB*).

[15] Slavoj Žižek, *The Puppet and the Dwarf: The Perverse Core of Christianity* (Short Circuits; Cambridge, MA: MIT Press, 2003) (henceforth cited as *PD*).

Slavoj Žižek

*Subject* (1999), *Did Somebody Say Totalitarianism?* (2001)[16] and *The Parallax View* (2006)[17] we can clearly discern this turn towards religion. However, this does not mean that religion is completely absent in his earlier work. On the contrary, as Kay points out, Žižek made use of overtly Christian thinkers like Kierkegaard, Pascal and Malebranche already in his earliest books. He also often refers to Hegel's discussion of the relationship between Greek, Jewish and Christian religion. Moreover the philosophers on whom he relies can be situated in the Protestant tradition.[18]

Nevertheless, Žižek's manner of dealing with Christianity has changed. While he used to refer to it mainly to illustrate another point, Christianity itself has now become the subject of analysis. Žižek describes himself as 'a Paulinian materialist'. By using this self-designation he wants to resist the postmodern understanding of religion that is adhered to by many contemporary thinkers and which implies that religion can only survive by leaving behind all ontological claims and converting into 'the respect and veneration of a kind of vacuous Otherness *à la* Levinas'. Žižek states that it is *not* 'the abstract messianic promise of some redemptive Otherness' that makes the Christian legacy worth fighting for, 'but, on the contrary, religion in its properly dogmatic and institutional aspect'. In a provocative way, he states that 'one can learn more from a Catholic conservative like Paul Claudel than from Levinas'.[19]

In what follows, we will investigate the Christological reflections offered by Žižek in his recent books (starting with *The Fragile Absolute*). This implies that the aim of the current chapter is rather limited. It does not intend to offer a comprehensive overview of the theme of religion in the work of Žižek because that does not fall within the scope of the present book. In this regard,

[16] Slavoj Žižek, *Did Somebody Say Totalitarianism? Five Interventions in the (Mis) Use of a Notion* (Wo es war; London and New York, NY: Verso, 2001) (henceforth cited as *DSST*).

[17] Slavoj Žižek, *The Parallax View* (Short Circuits; Cambridge, MA: MIT Press, 2006) (henceforth cited as *PV*).

[18] Kay, *Žižek*, p. 103.

[19] Žižek, 'Burning the Bridges', p. ix.

for instance, his reading of St Paul or his materialist theology of grace will not be dealt with.

## 2. Žižek's Lacanian Christology: Christ as the Ultimate *objet petit a*

### a. The Deadlock of the Sacrificial Interpretation of Christ's Death on the Cross

In the last pages of *The Fragile Absolute*, Žižek questions the traditional view according to which Christ, God's only-begotten son, died on the cross in order to redeem humanity. For, in this way, Christ's death on the cross is reduced to 'a sacrificial gesture in the exchange between God and man' and this immediately gives rise to some very disturbing questions: *Why* does God have to sacrifice his son? Is there maybe some higher authority or necessity above God with whom God has to comply in doing this? In that case, however, God can no longer be considered as omnipotent. God is then

> like a Greek tragic hero subordinated to a higher Destiny:
> His act of creation, like the fateful deed of the Greek hero,
> brings about unwanted dire consequences, and the only
> way for Him to re-establish the balance of Justice is to
> sacrifice what is most precious to Him, His own son.

On the other hand, when we want to hold on to God's omnipotence, the only possible conclusion seems that God is

> a *perverse* subject who plays obscene games with
> humanity and His own son: He creates suffering, sin
> and imperfection, so that He can intervene and resolve
> the mess He created, thereby securing for Himself the
> eternal gratitude of the human race (*FA* 157–58; see also
> *DSST* 45).

This dilemma is taken up again and elaborated upon in *Did Somebody Say Totalitarianism?*. If we consider Christ's death as ransoming our sins, *who* asked for a ransom in the first place? *Who* asked for such a heavy price? (1) *A first possibility* is that Christ's death is the ransom paid by God to the Devil, who owns those living in sin. This view, however, leads to 'the strange spectacle of God and the Devil as partners in an exchange'. (2) *A second possibility* is that God is the plaintiff. For, human sin has offended God's honour and that offended honour should be satisfied. Yet, humanity is not capable of providing this satisfaction on its own. Only God can and does so by sending his Son, Christ, the God-man. Being God, Christ is able to accomplish the required satisfaction; being human, he can replace us in doing so. This view has been defended by Anselm of Canterbury. It is, however, not without serious difficulties. Does it not turn God into a cruel, merciless and jealous creature? What kind of God demands such a bloody satisfaction merely because his honour has been offended by our sins? Moreover, why should God comply with the need to satisfy an offended honour? Why does God not simply forgive humanity *directly*, without having recourse to a bloody sacrifice? (3) This brings us to *a third possibility*, namely that God could indeed have forgiven us directly, but nevertheless sent us his son 'in order to set the ultimate example that would evoke our sympathy for him, and thus convert us to him'. This position has been adopted by Abelard, who stated that 'The Son of God took our nature, . . ., thus binding us to himself through love'. This, however, is not really a satisfying solution. For, as Žižek remarks:

> It is easy to see that something is amiss in this reasoning: is this not a strange God who sacrifices his own Son, what matters most to him, just to impress humans? Things become even more uncanny if we focus on the idea that God sacrificed his Son in order to bind us to himself through Love: what was at stake, then, was not only God's love for us, but also his (narcissistic) desire to *be loved* by us humans – in this reading, is not God himself strangely akin to the mad governess from Patricia Highsmith's 'Heroine', who sets the family house on fire in order to be able to prove her devotion to the family by bravely saving the children from the raging flames? Along these lines, God first causes the Fall (that is, provokes

a situation in which we need him) and then redeems us
(pulls us out of the mess for which he himself is responsible) (*DSST* 46–49).

This is 'the perverse core of Christianity' Žižek is referring to
in the sub-title of his *The Puppet and the Dwarf*. Indeed, how could
we fail to notice the perverse strategy of God in Genesis 2 and 3?
If God really wanted to avoid human sin, why put the Tree of the
Knowledge of Good-and-Evil in the Garden of Eden in the first
place? And where did the snake come from? One cannot avoid
the impression that the whole *mise en scène* was precisely aimed at
letting Adam and Eve sin, in order that God would be able to save
humanity later on through Christ's sacrifice (*PD* 15 and 53).

Moreover, as Žižek points out in *On Belief*, is Christianity not,
by explaining Christ's death on the cross as an 'inexplicable act of
Mercy, of paying our debt', burdening humanity with even more
guilt? One can of course react to this by stating that Christ is precisely *not* asking anything in return, because he has acted out of
love for humankind. Yet, is it not exactly 'through NOT demanding from us the price for our sins, through paying this price for us
Himself [through his Son], that the Christian God of Mercy estab-
lishes itself as the supreme superego agency: "I paid the highest
price for your sins, and you are thus indebted to me FOREVER
. . ."' (*OB* 144–45). Does an 'excess of mercy without proportion
to what I deserve' not automatically lead to an 'excess of guilt
without proportion to what I actually did' (*PD* 110)? And should
we not think in this regard of the example of the spouse who, during a domestic quarrel, answers to her desperate husband's question
'But what do you want from me?' with a firm 'Nothing!'? Is what
she means to say not that she wants nothing *in particular*? And is
she thus not saying the complete opposite of what she is actually
saying? Is she not asking 'for total surrender beyond any negoti-
ated element'? And is the same not true for Christ? For, as Žižek
puts it:

> When the falsely innocent Christlike figure of pure
> suffering and sacrifice for our sake tells us: "I don't want
> anything from you!," we can be sure that this statement
> conceals a qualification ". . . except *your very soul*." When

Slavoj Žižek

somebody insists that he [sic] wants nothing that we have,
it simply means that he has his eye on what we *are*, on the
very core of our being (*PD* 170).

It is however possible, according to Žižek, to offer an account
of Christianity that does not fall in the trap of this perversion. But
in this case we must abandon the idea that Christ's death was a
sacrifice. In what follows, we shall examine this alternative account
of Christianity.

## b. From God as 'Wholly Other Thing' to God as 'Barely Nothing'

In *On Belief* Žižek refers to the way science-fiction horror films
depict the alien. There are two different ways of doing so. On
the one hand, the alien can be depicted as 'wholly Other', as a
terrible Thing, 'a monster whose sight one cannot endure, usually
a mixture of reptile, octopus and machine'. On the other hand,
the aliens can also be 'EXACTLY THE SAME as we, ordinary
humans – with, of course, some "barely nothing" which allows us
to identify Them [as aliens] (the strange gleam in their eyes; too
much skin between their fingers . . .)' (*OB* 131). According to
Žižek, it is precisely this difference between the alien as a 'wholly
Other Thing' and the alien who is almost completely identical to
ordinary humans, except for some 'barely nothing', that acts as a
heuristic for understanding the difference between the God of
Judaism and the God of Christianity.

In Judaism, God is, according to Žižek, 'the transcendent irrep-
resentable Other'. Judaism states that the suprasensible dimension
(the Sublime) is beyond the sensible, is the 'Real behind the
curtain of the phenomena', and it tries to render that Real precisely by renouncing all images (*OB* 89). To elaborate on this, we
can refer to Žižek's discussion (first in *The Fragile Absolute* [103–
04] and elaborated in *On Belief*) of the Jewish iconoclasm, its
prohibition of making images of God. It is important, however,
not to misunderstand this iconoclasm. It is commonplace to state
that pagan gods were anthropomorphic, while the Jews were the
first to thoroughly de-anthropomorphize their God. According
to this view, images of God are prohibited because they 'would

"humanize" [a] purely spiritual Entity'. According to Žižek, however, this view is not correct. Pagans did *not* believe their images
to be gods and they did not even believe these images to be, in
any way, adequate representations of the gods. And this is why
iconoclasm can never make sense for paganism. Images of the
gods are neither true nor adequate anyway. So, the Jewish prohibition of making images of God can, according to Žižek, only be
intelligible when we assume that the Jews believed that such
an image

> would show too much, rendering visible some horrifying
> secret better left in shadow, WHICH IS WHY THEY
> HAD TO PROHIBIT IT – the Jewish prohibition
> only makes sense against the background of this fear
> that the image would reveal something shattering, that,
> in an unbearable way, it would be TRUE and ADEQUATE
> (*OB* 129–30 and 132).

But what 'horrifying secret' would have emerged, had the
Jews made images of their God? To trace this secret, we should
state, Žižek claims in contrast to the common view, that in fact the
Jews completely personalized and anthropomorphized God. Their
God is just 'another PERSON in the fullest sense of the term'.
Indeed, 'the Jewish God experiences full wrath, revengefulness,
jealousy, etc., as every human being'. Thus, Jewish iconoclasm
should be understood, not as a reaction to previous pagan religiosity, but as a necessary consequence of Judaism's own full
personalization of God. For, an image 'would render [the Jewish
God] all too faithfully, as the ultimate Neighbor-Thing' and the
Jewish iconoclasm is precisely aimed at avoiding this traumatic
experience of God as just another person (*OB* 130–31).

According to Žižek, it is in Christianity that the secret of
Judaism is brought to light 'by asserting not only the likeness
of God and man, but their direct *identity* in the figure of
Christ'. So, Christianity completes the personalization of God
already begun but not fully completed by Judaism. It accepts God
'as JUST ANOTHER HUMAN BEING, as a miserable man
indiscernible from other humans with regard to his intrinsic

properties'.[20] In this way, only Christianity really escapes from paganism, really 'sublates' it, while Judaism still 'remains an "abstract/immediate" negation of anthropomorphism, and, as such, attached to it, determined by it in its very direct negation' (*OB* 131). Or, to put it differently, Christianity rejects the 'God of Beyond' and can thus be described as a radical desublimation, 'in the sense of the descendence of the sublime Beyond to the everyday level'. So, Christianity makes the transition from God as 'the wholly Other Thing' to the Divine as 'barely nothing', as 'the imperceptible "something" [that makes Christ divine], a pure appearance which cannot ever be grounded in a substantial property'. But what is this 'barely nothing' – this 'imperceptible something'? Or, to phrase it differently: what is the Divine? (*OB* 89–90) In order to answer these questions, we now turn to Žižek's view on what exactly makes us *human* beings rather than just another animal species.

## c. An Excess of Life that Makes Us Human

In *The Ticklish Subject*, Žižek discusses the transition from nature to culture – from the human being as 'a mere animal' to the human being as 'a "being of language"', bound by symbolic Law'. According to Žižek, we should reject the common sense view, in which the Law aims at controlling our natural passions and inclinations. Rather, the Law is directed, *not* against our natural instincts, but against something completely *unnatural*, against 'a moment of thoroughly "perverted", "denaturalized", "derailed" nature which is not yet culture'. Thus, there is no smooth, evolutionary development from nature to culture. On the contrary, the transition from nature to culture is brought about by something that is no longer nature but is also not yet culture. This 'vanishing mediator', this

[20] This is further illustrated by Žižek, in his typical style, with some references to movies: '[Christ] is fully human, inherently indistinguishable from other humans in exactly the same way Judy is indistinguishable from Madeleine in [Hitchcock's] *Vertigo*, or the "true" Erhardt is indistinguishable from his impersonator in [Alan Johnson's] *To Be Or Not To Be* [1983] – [. . .]' (*OB* 90).

'In-between', is nothing more and nothing less than *the appearance of the drive* (*TS* 36–37).

It is important to keep in mind the distinction, made by Freud, between 'drive' (German: *Trieb*) and 'instinct' (German: *Instinkt*). *Instincts* are biological needs, such as the need to eat, drink and copulate. As Dylan Evans states in his *Introductory Dictionary of Lacanian Psychoanalysis*, instincts have 'a relatively fixed and innate relationship to an object'. Their most distinguishing characteristic is that they can be satisfied by, for instance: eating, drinking or copulating. The *drives*, in contrast, are not linked to a particular object. They 'differ from biological needs in that they can never be satisfied, and do not aim at an object but rather circle perpetually round it.'[21] This distinction between biological needs and drives – or to put it differently, the distinction between animal and human being – can be clarified further with the help of one of Žižek's favourite anecdotes concerning a laboratory experiment with rats, once described by Jacques-Alain Miller, son-in-law and self-proclaimed heir of Lacan:

> [I]n a labyrinthine set-up, a desired object [actually an object of biological need] (a piece of good food or a sexual partner) is first made easily accessible to a rat; then, the set-up is changed in such a way that the rat sees and thereby knows where the desired object is, but cannot gain access to it; in exchange for it, as a kind of consolation prize, a series of similar objects of inferior value is made easily accessible – how does the rat react to it? For some time, it tries to find its way to the "true" object; then, upon ascertaining that this object is definitely out of reach, the rat will renounce it and [put up with] some of the inferior substitute objects – in short, it will act as a "rational" subject of utilitarianism. It is only now, however, that the true experiment begins: the scientists performed a surgical operation on the rat, messing about with its brain, doing things to it with laser beams about which, as Miller put it delicately, it is better to know nothing.

---

[21] Dylan Evans, *An Introductory Dictionary of Lacanian Psychoanalysis* (repr., London and New York, NY: Routledge, 1997) p. 46.

So what happened when the operated rat was again let loose in the labyrinth, the one in which the "true" object is inaccessible? *The rat insisted*: it never became fully reconciled to the loss of the "true" object and [never] resigned itself to one of the inferior substitutes, but repeatedly returned to the "true" object and attempted to reach it. In short, the rat in a sense was *humanized*, it assumed the tragic "human" relationship towards the unattainable absolute object which, on account of its very inaccessibility, forever captivates our desire. (Miller's point, of course, is that this quasi-humanization of the rat resulted from its biological *mutilation*: the unfortunate rat started to act like a human being in relationship to its object of desire when its brain was butchered and crippled by means of an "unnatural" surgical intervention.) On the other hand, it is this very "conservative" fixation that pushes man to continuing renovation, since he never can fully integrate this excess into his life process. So we can see why Freud used the term "death drive": the lesson of psychoanalysis is that humans are not simply alive but are possessed by a strange drive to enjoy life in excess of the ordinary run of things – and "death" stands simply and precisely for the dimension beyond ordinary biological life (*OB* 103–04).[22]

To sum up, in the first part of the experiment the rat is 'a mere animal' looking for objects that can satisfy its biological needs (food, a partner). When confronted with an object that would meet these needs in a very satisfactory way, but that is inaccessible,

---

[22] See also p. 102: 'Life thus loses its tautological self-satisfactory evidence: it comprises an excess which disturbs its balanced run.' It becomes:

> marked/stained by an excess, containing a "remainder" which no longer fits the simple life process. "To live" no longer means to pursue the balanced process of reproduction, but to get "passionately attached" or stuck to some excess, to some kernel of the Real, whose role is contradictory: it introduces the aspect of fixity or "fixation" into the life process – man is ultimately an animal whose life is derailed through the excessive fixation to some traumatic Thing (pp. 102–03).

> As a result, 'Human life is never "just life," it is always sustained by an excess of life' (p. 104).

the rat simply renounces the object and is content with another object, even if it is less satisfying. In the second part of the experiment, after the rat has been 'humanized', by messing about with its brain, it shows, in contrast, 'a stubborn attachment' to the impossible object. The object in question has become a Thing, something to which the rat is excessively attached. The rat comes back to its Thing again and again, trying to reach it nevertheless. And precisely this endless repetition of the same failed gesture, this 'closed loop', is the drive.

*The drive is thus not to be understood as a remainder of animal nature* in human persons, lurking under a small layer of civilization imposed on them by the Law of culture, but still ready to take over control again in a moment of unattentiveness. *On the contrary, the drive should be understood as thoroughly unnatural.* The rat only enters the domain of the drive *after* its brain has been messed up, *after* some malicious experiment allowed the smooth course of spontaneous, biological life to derail. *The drive is an 'excessive love of freedom, . . .,* which goes far beyond obeying animal instincts'. The drive is 'an uncanny "unruliness" that seems to be inherent in human nature', 'a wild unconstrained propensity to insist stubbornly on one's own will, cost what it may' (*TS* 36–37).

*The Law of culture aims at pacifying this 'excessive love of freedom' and at returning to a new kind of 'naturalness',* namely that of culture, which is the actual nature of human beings. The Law prohibits the Thing, the impossible object of full satisfaction, and introduces in this way the metonymy of desire (see Figure 1 below, in which *d* stands for desire and $ is the Lacanian notation for the subject). The closed loop of the drive, the endless circular course around the impossible object, is forced open and replaced by a succession of substitutes for the forbidden Thing. In this way, closure is replaced by radical openness. For, since the satisfaction obtained by a substitute

[23] Or as Žižek puts it:

> [T]he ultimate function of the symbolic Law is to enable us to AVOID the debilitating deadlock of drive – the symbolic Law already reacts to a certain inherent impediment on account of which the animal instinct somehow gets "stuck" and explodes in the excessive repetitive moment, it enables the subject to magically transform this repetitive movement through which the subject is stuck *with* and *for* the drive's cause-object, into the eternal open search for the (lost/prohibited) object of desire (*OB* 97–98).

Slavoj Žižek

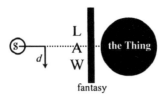

**Figure 1** Existence under the Law: the metonymy of desire.

always fails miserably in comparison to the satisfaction expected from the Thing, the succession of desired objects is endless.[23]

*This transition from drive to desire*, effected by the Law of the symbolic order, *is, on the one hand, a return to a kind of naturalness*, since – as has been indicated above – also the rat as mere animal quickly turned to substitutes and this brought Žižek to the remark that in that case the rat acted 'as a "rational" subject of utilitarianism'. *On the other hand, however, the naturalness installed by the Law is not a return to spontaneous animal life.* Human desire is not a return to biological need. The humanized animal does not really give up its Thing and remains stubbornly attached to it (as expressed by the dotted line in the figure). Moreover, *the course of desire is sustained by the illusion that full satisfaction* (the possession of the Thing) *would be possible if only the Law did not prevent it.* Or, to put it differently, the Law calls into being the fantasy that the Thing is not really impossible, but only forbidden and fosters in this way the expectation that one day possession of the Thing will become possible. It is this expectation which *drives* human culture and has caused human evolution's ever accelerating pace, while the chimpanzees – our closest relatives in the animal kingdom, with whom we share more than 98 per cent of our genetic material – have almost remained unaltered for the past six million years.

Furthermore, *the Law is not able to prevent a resurgence of the drive.* In contrast to biological need and like the drive, desire is not linked to particular objects. Anything can become an object of human desire; which is demonstrated by the fact that human beings can become addicted to anything, be it cigarettes, coffee, chocolate, gambling, porn or even collecting stamps (the so-called 'universalization of addiction' [*OB* 102]). These addictions make clear that human beings desire beyond what is necessary to survive and even beyond what is necessary to live a pleasurable life.

Humans can even desire at the expense of their well-being. Cigarettes, coffee and chocolate are bad for one's health. Cigarettes, gambling and porn cost bags of money. Gambling can ruin one financially and porn can destroy one's marriage and social life. Although addicts *know* all this and often experience the unpleasant consequences of their addiction, they simply cannot give up their bad habit. This makes it clear that striving for pleasure (German: *Lust*) is not the primary principle in human life.

*The pleasure principle*, which dictates our daily functioning, implies that human beings strive for pleasure and avoid pain. It is installed by the Law of the symbolic order and *aims at restoring the bond between desire and object*, a bond which was lost when biological need derailed as drive. The pleasure principle forbids pursuing our desire just like that and states that we should take consequences into account. It states that we should always make a rational calculation of costs and benefits. As Freud himself as already made clear with his reality principle (which is – in contrast to common opinion – not contrary to the pleasure principle, but on the contrary a part of it), it can be better to renounce a pleasure in the short term, to avoid pain or obtain a greater pleasure in the long term. *The pleasure principle*, however, *does not succeed in completely mastering the excessiveness of human desire.* Human beings can always go 'beyond the pleasure principle', to use the title of Freud's famous 1920 essay. Beyond the pleasure principle lies the domain of the Thing – that Thing for which we are prepared to sacrifice everything: all we posses, our well-being and even our very life. It is the domain of *jouissance* (German: *Genuß*), of an excessive enjoyment in pain beyond all limits that is no longer pleasant in the ordinary sense of the term.

Entering the domain beyond the pleasure principle, however, implies the end of the human being as a symbolic subject, as a

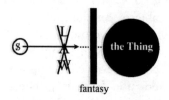

fantasy

**Figure 2**   The death drive: addiction and transgression.

being of language, which, as desiring, only exists in its distance from the Thing and which is that distance.[24] Therefore, entering the domain of the Thing is lethal. Nevertheless, in *Beyond the Pleasure Principle*, Freud identified the death drive, the drive towards the lethal Thing, as the primary force in human life. The symbolic Law and language, pleasure and desire are all secondary phenomena: defences against the unbearable *jouissance* of the Thing to which the death drive drives us. As can be seen in Figure 2, the death drive is essentially transgressive and aims at reaching the *jouissance* of the Thing by eliminating the Law.

The transgressor, however, runs the risk of getting stuck in what we can (in Hegelian terms) describe as 'a bad infinity'. He or she will need ever greater transgressions to experience the same effect. It is as with a drug addict who always needs greater doses and it is the same with the novels of the notorious Marquis the Sade, which report an endless repetition of transgressions. In this way, the endless metonymy of desire has only been replaced by another endlessness. Moreover, the transgressor is actually still attached to the Law. For, he/she finds *jouissance* − *not* in reaching the Thing (which always remains elusive) − but precisely in transgressing the Law. This is due to the fact that, though the transgressor breaks the Law, its hidden foundation, namely fantasy, remains operative and therefore the perpetrator is still victim to the illusion that the Thing is only inaccessible because it is forbidden by the Law and that it suffices to go beyond the Law to possess it.

## d. The Coming of Christ: The Death of the Divine Thing

Our discussion in the previous subsection seems to imply that we are forced to choose between two possibilities: on the one hand,

---

[24] This is formulated by Marc De Kesel as follows:

> The 'being of pleasure' may then go back to an identification with an object, simultaneously it only lives by (and *as*) the distance that it keeps from it. [. . .] The function of the 'thing' is thus as paradoxical as double: it shows how the 'being of pleasure' *is both* its object *and* its relation to that object (Marc De Kesel, *Eros & ethiek: Een lectuur van Jacques Lacans Séminaire VII* (Psychoanalyse in tijden van wetenschap, 1; Leuven and Leusden: Acco, 2002) pp. 115–16 [my translation]).

tragic desire and dull pleasure under the reign of the Law and, on the other, lethal transgression of the Law towards the domain of the Thing (with its promise of unlimited *jouissance*, which, however, always remains unfulfilled; because, beyond the Law, full satisfaction remains inaccessible). Yet, is this not similar to the choice between pestilence and cholera? According to Žižek, thankfully, there are yet other possibilities and it is precisely in this regard that the above-mentioned transition from God as 'the wholly other Thing' to the Divine as 'barely nothing' becomes the prime example.

But before we turn to this, we should first explain another Lacanian category, namely the *objet petit a* (or 'object little *a*', but Lacan insisted that it should not be translated). In order to do this, we have to take up 'the Thing' again. As we have already seen, *the Thing*, being the impossible/forbidden object in which desire would find complete satisfaction, *is nothing but its own absence*: it is a hole in the centre of the symbolic order around which that order turns. In that empty space, however, objects can appear, which are – simply because they are in that empty space where the Thing is lacking – 'raised to the dignity of the Thing' (this being the Lacanian formula for sublimation). These objects are designated by Lacan as *objets petit a*. Traditionally, there are four such objects, namely the breast, the faeces, the voice and the gaze. According to Žižek, however, everything can be become an *objet petit a* and, as such, an 'incarnation' of (the lack) of the Thing. Or, as he puts it:

> [T]he Thing is nothing but its own lack, the elusive spectre of the lost primordial object of desire engendered by the symbolic Law/Prohibition, and *l'objet petit a* . . . mediates between the a priori void of the impossible Thing and the empirical objects that give us (dis)pleasure – *objets a* are empirical objects contingently elevated to the dignity of the Thing, so that they start to function as embodiments of the impossible Thing (*OB* 97).

However, it is more correct to speak, as Philippe Van Haute does in his *Against Adaptation*, about the *objet petit a* as the 'dis-incarnation, as it were, of the lack'. For, on the one hand, it indeed

110

gives a concrete, bodily filling-in of the absence of the Thing (incarnation), but on the other hand it remains forever elusive (dis-incarnation).[25]

*All this enables us to elaborate further on the difference between paganism, Judaism and Christianity.* Both paganism and Judaism believe in a suprasensible plenitude beyond the symbolic order. As we have already seen above, pagans do not believe their idols to be adequate representations of the gods. Nevertheless, they try to grasp something of the suprasensible dimension through creating a multitude of images, or, as Žižek puts it, 'through the overwhelming excess of the sensible, like the Indian statues with dozens of hands'. Judaism, in contrast, renounces all images together and 'tries to render the suprasensible dimension' precisely in this way (*OB* 89). So, to formulate it differently, while the pagans seek comfort for the absence of the Thing and the harshness of the symbolic Law by having recourse to the imaginary, such a consolation is refused to the Jews. They keep open the space between themselves and the Law (the space which is filled-up by paganism with imaginary constructions). In this way, however, they are directly confronted with the Law in all its arbitrariness, as is depicted in Figure 3 below.

Both pagans and Jews, however, share the belief in a sublime beyond. To put it differently, they both believe in God as the Thing and thus both share the fantasy that the Divine Thing is far too sublime, far too elevated for human beings to be able to handle direct confrontation with it.

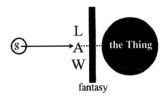

**Figure 3**   The Jewish relationship to the suprasensible dimension.

[25] Philippe Van Haute, *Against Adaptation: Lacan's Subversion of the Subject* (trans. Paul Crowe *et al.*; The Lacanian Clinical Field; New York, NY: Other Press, 2002) p. 151.

*The coming of Christ now implies the death of this Divine Thing.* In Christ, as we have already seen, the Divine is, according to Žižek, reduced to 'the pure *Schein* of another dimension' (*OB* 89), to something in Christ that is more than himself. This 'something' is nothing more and nothing less than the surplus 'on account of which man cannot ever fully become MAN, self-identical'. So, according to Žižek, the Divine is *not* 'the Highest in man, the purely spiritual dimension towards which all humans strive', *not* some inaccessible/prohibited sublime plenitude beyond the world of visible phenomena. Beyond the phenomena, there is nothing, 'nothing BUT the imperceptible X that changes Christ, this ordinary man, into God'. This X, however, is precisely the excess of human life, that 'too much' that makes us into humans (and not mere animals), but can never be contained within smooth biological life. The Divine is nothing but the obstacle that makes us human, simultaneously preventing our ever becoming self-identical. In this way, we are now able to understand 'the ABSOLUTE identity of man and God' which is, according to Žižek, proclaimed by Christianity: the Divine is nothing more and nothing less than that which makes us human beings instead of mere animals and this is what has been revealed by Christ (*OB* 89 and 90–91).[26]

*In this way, the coming of Christ does imply the end of the 'God of Beyond'.* In this regard, Žižek speaks, as we have already mentioned, about desublimation: 'the descendence of the sublime Beyond to the everyday level' (*OB* 90) or 'the coincidence, identity even, between the sublime and the everyday object' (*OB* 92). *This corresponds to a transition from the Thing to the* objet petit a, *and from desire to drive.* As we have seen, desire thrives under the

---

[26] According to Žižek, this entails that we should not understand Christ as possessing two substances Or, as he puts it in *The Parallax View*:

[Christ], in contrast to previous pagan divinities, does not "represent" some universal power our principle [. . .]: as this miserable human, Christ directly is God. Christ is not *also* human, apart from being God; he is a man precisely *insofar as he is God*; that is, the *ecce homo* is the highest mark of his divinity.

In this regard, Žižek adds, Pilate's 'Ecce homo!' means nothing more and nothing less than 'Here is God himself!' (*PV* 105–06).

Law, which forbids the impossible Thing and installs the distance to the Thing, the distance *which is* the subject of desire. The logic of desire is indeed based on placing an impossible Thing in an inaccessible Beyond as forbidden. Desire is the endless movement from one substitute to the next, without ever reaching an end. Therefore, desire is inherently tragic: every substitute is not It. Or, as Žižek puts it, 'the *obtained* satisfaction' never equals 'the *sought-for* satisfaction' and it is precisely in this gap that desire thrives (*OB* 90). As we have already said repeatedly, this subject position is sustained by the fantasy that the Thing is not impossible as such, but only because it is forbidden by the Law.

*The coming of Christ*, however, *traverses this fantasy*: the Divine Thing does not exist and it is only its own absence, nothing but an empty space. In this way we are able *to leave the domain of tragic desire behind and to (re-)enter the domain of drive*. The drive clings to some particular – 'pathological' (in the Kantian sense of the word) – object that is also the support of something in the object that is more than the object itself and that we can designate, in Lacanian terms, as the *objet petit a*. The domain of drive is also the one of love. Love precisely consists in the identification of some 'very clumsy and miserable being' as the locus from which another dimension shines forth. Žižek puts this as follows: 'Love [in contrast to desire] FULLY ACCEPTS that "this IS that" – that the woman with all her weaknesses and common features IS the Thing I unconditionally love' (*OB* 90). Love thus means that something, for instance the body of one's partner, 'starts to function as the object around which drive circulates' (*OB* 94).[27] This is

---

[27] Yet, it is important to understand Žižek correctly:

> [T]his does NOT mean that [the partner's] ordinary ("pathological," in the Kantian sense of the term) flesh-and-blood body is "transubstantiated" into a contingent embodiment of the sublime impossible Thing, holding (filling out) its empty place. [. . .], what makes [the material support of the *objet petit a*] an "infinitely" desirable object whose "mystery" cannot ever be fully penetrated, is its non-identity to itself, i.e. the way it is never directly "itself." The gap which "eternalizes" drive, turning it into the endlessly repetitive circular movement around the object, is not the gap that separates the void of the Thing from its contingent embodiments, but the gap that separates the very "pathological" object FROM ITSELF (*OB* 94–95).

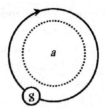

**Figure 4**   Drive and love.

shown in Figure 4 in which the circle in the dotted line stands for the material support of the *objet petit a* and the outer circle stands for the drive, the circular movement of the subject around this spectral object.

Žižek thus concludes that, *while Judaism is the religion of desire, Christianity is the religion of love.* Judaism *desires* for God, who, precisely as the Sublime Beyond, remains inaccessible. Yet, according to Žižek, the coming of Christ does not imply that we simply renounce transcendence completely. On the contrary, in Him, *the transcendent realm becomes accessible as 'immanent transcendence'* (*OB* 99). Christ is not merely a stand-in for God, not one substitute for the impossible Divine Thing among many possibilities. He is not a 'contingent material ("pathological") embodiment of the suprasensible God'. *Christ is God.* With his coming, the 'God of Beyond' has died and the Divine is reduced to nothing but 'the aura of a pure *Schein*' that shines through this fellow human being (*OB* 95).[28] But precisely in this way it becomes accessible for our attachment *in love.*

---

[28] This implies, as Žižek had put in *The Fragile Absolute*, that the sentimental cliché, according to which we can discern God's face in every human face which expresses benevolence and goodness, is actually true:

> The truth of this sentimental platitude is that the Suprasensible (God's face) is discernible as a momentary, fleeting appearance, a 'grimace', of an earthly face. It is in *this* sense (an 'appearance' which, as it were, transubstantiates a piece of reality into something that, for a brief moment, radiates the suprasensible Eternity) that man is like God: in both cases, the structure is that of an *appearance*, of a sublime dimension that *appears through* the sensible image of the face – or as Lacan puts it, following Hegel, the suprasensible is [nothing but] the appearance as such ... (*FA* 104–05).

## e. 'Father, Why Did You Forsake Me?'

The transition from Judaism to Christianity can also be put in terms of a transition from 'the enigma *of*' to 'the enigma *in*'. Both in *Did Somebody Say Totalitarianism?* and in *On Belief*, Žižek refers in this regard to a famous phrase from Hegel who stated that 'The enigmas of the Ancient Egyptians were also enigmas for the Egyptians themselves'. Applying this idea to the wholly other, Divine Thing, the '*Dieu obscur*', 'the elusive, impenetrable God' of Judaism, Žižek concludes that this God has to be a mystery for himself. He 'must also be impenetrable to himself; he must have a dark side, an Otherness in himself, something that is in himself more than himself'. This, Žižek continues, accounts for the incarnation. Christ had to appear, not to reveal God to humankind, but to reveal God to himself (*DSST* 56–57; *OB* 145).

According to Žižek, it is precisely God being an enigma for himself which is the novelty of Christianity in comparison with pre-Christian religiosity. This mystery of God for himself culminates in the words of Jesus on the cross: 'Father, why did you forsake me?' At that moment, God is completely abandoned by God and thus shares the human experience of being abandoned by God. In this way, it is the moment when 'Christ becomes FULLY human', the moment when '*the radical gap that separates God from man is transposed into God Himself*'. On the cross, God abandons himself totally and in this way the absolute identity of God and humankind is realized. Or, as Žižek puts it: '*When I, a human being, experience myself as cut off from God, at that very moment of the utmost abjection, I am absolutely close to God, since I find myself in the position of the abandoned Christ.*'[29] Moreover, the Crucifixion is, Žižek adds, the moment when God discovers the limits of his

---

[29] Cf. *PV* 106:

> In Christianity, the gap that separates God from man is not directly "sublated" in the figure of Christ as God-man; it is rather that, in the most tense moment of crucifixion, when Christ himself despairs ("Father, why have you forsaken me?"), the gap that separates God from man is transposed into God himself, as the gap that separates Christ from God-Father; the properly dialectical trick here is that the very feature which appeared to separate me from God turns out to unite me with God.

omnipotence (*OB* 146; see also *PD* 14–15). The fact that God is a mystery for himself suggests that God is not perfect. It is only this imperfection of God, however, which makes true Christian love possible. According to Žižek, we can only love an Other insofar as that Other is not perfect. Or, as he had already put it in *Did Somebody Say Totalitarianism?*, 'love is always love for the Other in so far as he is lacking – we love the Other *because* of his limitations. The radical conclusion from this is that, if God is to be loved, he must be *imperfect*, . . .' (*DSST* 57; *OB* 146–47).

The idea of divine self-abandonment is elaborated upon in *The Puppet and the Dwarf* with the help of a discussion of the story of Job. Žižek already mentions Job in *On Belief*, in which he states that the Christian answer to the story of Job consists in God taking the place of a God-forsaken man (*OB* 146). In *The Puppet and the Dwarf*, he adds that Job offers us the key to a correct understanding of the Crucifixion. The transition from Job to Christ stands for the change from Judaism to Christianity. Job is a human being confronted with the mystery of an impenetrable and incomprehensible Divine Thing (*PD* 124). In the crucified Jesus, God occupies the place of Job: he is abandoned by himself and discovers his own impenetrability, his own impotence. This enables Žižek to compare the experience of Christ on the cross with the one of a child that discovers his/her father's powerlessness and he continues by evoking an example from recent history:

> At the moment of Christ's Crucifixion, God-the-Father
> is in a position somewhat similar to that of the Bosnian
> father, made to witness the gang-rape of his own daughter,
> and to endure the ultimate trauma of her compassionate-
> reproachful gaze: "Father, why did you forsake me?"
> (*PD* 125–26)

In fact, Žižek further explains, God's impotence was already inscribed in the story of Job without being made explicit. Indeed, is not the most disturbing element of that story the way God reacts to Job by boasting and pure display of power? This suggests that God is actually overreacting, that he vents his rage upon poor Job because he has in fact been caught by him in a moment of utter weakness and impotence. The 'cheap Hollywood horror show with lots of special effects' which we get at the end of the story is then merely an attempt of God to hide that weakness again (*PD* 124–25). And is Job's silence at the end of the story not a gesture of utter solidarity and pity with the God which he has just discovered as impotent and pitiful? (*PD* 126–27). This brings Žižek back once more to the difference between Judaism and Christianity: in Judaism, God's utter impotence is kept as a horrifying secret, while in Christianity this secret is brought to light, is 'revealed' (*PD* 129). Therefore, Christianity is truly the 'revealed religion', because there is nothing left behind, there are no secrets anymore, God's impotence has been divulged (*PD* 127). In Žižek's view, however, the disclosure of divine powerlessness amounts to the death of God-the-Father (*PD* 126). In this regard, Christianity turns out to be truly 'the religion of atheism' (*PD* 171). On the cross, God no longer believes in himself and thus becomes an atheist (*PD* 14; *PV* 352). Or, as Žižek puts it: '[I]n Christianity, God dies *for Himself*. In his "Father, why hast thou forsaken me?," Christ himself commits what is, for a Christian, the ultimate sin: he wavers in his Faith' (*PD* 15). Or, as Žižek puts it on the final page of *The Puppet and the Dwarf*: 'When Christ dies, what dies with him is the secret hope discernible in "Father, why hast thou forsaken me?": the hope that there is a father who has abandoned me' (*PD* 171). Elsewhere in *The Puppet and the Dwarf*, Žižek speaks in this respect about God falling into creation, becoming included in 'the series of ordinary creatures' (*PD* 136, 137, 138) and insofar as God is 'the ultimate Other', this entails to 'the suspension of Otherness', the reduction of Otherness to Sameness. God has become 'just one of us' (*PD* 138).

## f. The Crucified Christ: The Ultimate *objet petit a*

As stated in subsection a above, Žižek firmly rejects the sacrificial interpretation of Christ's death as 'perverse'. Yet, according to him, it is possible to offer a non-perverse reading of this event. In the light of our discussion in the previous subsections, we should now be able to formulate this alternative explanation. Therefore we should go back to the story of the Fall already mentioned in sub-section a above. According to Žižek, in Genesis, 'Paradise' stands for human life not yet contaminated by its excess; 'sin' is then precisely this 'excess of Life which makes [us] human' and the 'Fall' is the moment when 'the human animal contracted [this] excess' (*OB* 105).[30]

To clarify the way Christ relates to this excess, Žižek makes use of a comparison, which demonstrates that also his Marxist back-ground plays a role in his interpretation of Christ. His comparison is the following: Christ is among human beings what money is among ordinary commodities. A commodity should be carefully distinguished from a mere object (see for what follows, Table 1 below). An object belongs to the realm of nature and possesses a certain use value (for satisfying biological needs). A commodity, in contrast, is an object of symbolic exchange in the market. It has acquired a certain surplus value (or excess) through the labour invested in it. This surplus value is expressed in an amount of money. Money, however, is an exceptional object/commodity because it is without use value (outside of the symbolic exchange of the market it is completely useless – thinking about the benefit of money in surviving on a deserted island suffices in demonstrat-ing this claim). Nevertheless, and precisely in this vain, it enables

**Table 1** Money among the commodities

| Pre-symbolic Nature | Excess | Order of Symbolic Exchange |
|---|---|---|
| objects with use value (satisfying biological needs) | surplus value (< labour) → MONEY | commodities |
| money = material object without use value | money = incarnation of surplus value | money = commodity as such |

[30] See also in *The Puppet and the Dwarf*, p. 22: 'Original Sin [is] the abyssal disturbance of primeval Peace, the primordial "pathological" Choice of unconditional attachment to some specific object (like falling in love with a specific person who, thereafter, matters to us more than anything else.'

the symbolic exchange. As a result, money is 'the commodity "as such"': the incarnation of surplus value uncontaminated by use value and, therefore, 'the universal equivalent [that] exchanges/gives itself for all other excesses' (*OB* 99–100).

Table 2 below then makes clear in which way Christ is among human beings what money is among ordinary commodities. As money is the material substratum to which the excess that is surplus value (which is in itself nothing but an 'aura' of some 'incorporeal dimension') attaches itself, Christ is the material support for an incarnation of the excess of human life. He 'directly embodies/assumes the excess that makes the human animal a proper human being'. And as 'money is the commodity "as such"', Christ is man "as such"' (*OB* 99–100).

The question remains, however, of what the equivalent of money as 'material object without use value' could be in the second table. What is Christ within pre-symbolic nature? If we just follow the example of money, we should state something like 'Christ = a human animal without some X'. But what does X stand for? Žižek is not very clear on this point (and maybe he did not even have the intention to stretch his comparison as far as we are attempting to do here – but because we should always be attentive for what is *not* said, as psychoanalysis teaches us, the question is worth asking). Although Žižek is not clear, he gives us some clues. For instance, he states that Christ 'was the Pure one, without excess, simplicity itself' (*OB* 100). Žižek seemingly implies Christ was without the excess of life that characterizes humanity. Is Žižek translating here the orthodox view that Christ was without sin? This conclusion seems justified on the basis of

**Table 2**  Christ among human beings

| Pre-symbolic Nature | Excess | Order of Symbolic Exchange |
|---|---|---|
| human animals | an excess of life (< appearance of the drive) → CHRIST | human 'beings of language' |
| Christ = ? | Christ = incarnation the excess of human life (Christ = God) | Christ = man as such |

Žižek's interpretation of the story of the Fall, already mentioned above, where he interpreted 'sin' as 'the excess of life'. Yet, since this excess is precisely what turns the human animal into a human 'being of language', does this not imply that Žižek is actually saying that Christ was not a real human being? But maybe ortho-dox Christianity is implicitly doing the same when it states that Christ 'in every respect has been tested as we are, yet without sin' (Heb. 4.15). Yet, what is a human being without sin, without his/her constitutive excess? Merely an animal again? But how seri-ously can we take Žižek if he would be really claiming that Christ was merely a human animal?[31]

To elaborate further on this point, we can take up Žižek's statement that 'Christ as man = God is the unique case of full humanity' (OB 91). If Christ is a fulfilled or completed human being, he should indeed be without excess, for, as has already been repeatedly indicated, that excess is precisely the obstacle 'on account of which man cannot ever fully become MAN, self-identical' (OB 90). But does this necessarily imply a return to pre-symbolic nature? What if, in fact, it is rather the opposite? This is indeed what Žižek seems to imply: that Christ is the first case of a thoroughly denaturalized human being. In this way, the relationship between Adam's Fall and the Redemption brought by Christ, the Second Adam, appears in a completely new light. The Fall is not a pitiful incident, but already the first act of redemp-tion. Moreover, the coming of Christ is not aimed at rectifying the effects of the Fall, but at fulfilling them. The Fall is the first step on the way from human animal to full humanity. After the Fall, however, humanity remains stuck at the level of a negation of nature. It is only in Christ, the first case of full humanity, that the human animal is completely 'sublated' (PD 86–88, 118; PV 96–97; see also: TS 70–71). Therefore, Christ is, as Žižek puts

---

[31] Moreover, even in that case the comparison to money seemingly does not hold good. For, within pre-symbolic nature, money is less than other objects (it has no use value). Christ, in contrast, does not seem to lack anything within the realm of pre-symbolic nature. So the conclusion seems justified that Christ is not completely as money, or is it not?

it in *The Puppet and the Dwarf*, 'more than man'. In this regard, he even makes an explicit reference to Nietzsche's *Übermensch*:

> [A]nd why should we not take the risk here of referring to Nietzsche: [Christ] is *overman*? – precisely insofar as one can say, apropos of his figure: "Ecce homo," precisely insofar as he is a man *kat' exochen*, "as such," a man with no distinctions, no particular features.

Or, to put it with the title of a novel by Robert Musil, Christ is 'the ultimate *Mann ohne Eigenschaften*', 'the man without properties' (*PD* 80).

However, in what way can we understand that Christ was 'a man without properties'? Was he not, in contrast, a particular human being who said and did very particular things? Yet, maybe, we can make sense of Žižek's statements when we apply what he is saying to the moment of the Crucifixion. For at that moment, a particular human being was stripped of all his particular characteristics and reduced to 'man "as such"' (*OB* 100). At that moment, he had been disgorged by the symbolic order (he had already died symbolically, so to speak, he dwelt in what Lacan designated as 'the domain between the two deaths') and therefore he was reduced to nothing but a piece of waste, the excrement of the symbolic order. To elaborate on this, we can refer to *The Parallax View*, where Žižek falls back on Luther's idea of humankind as 'divine shit' that 'fell out of God's anus'. In this regard, Christ turns out to be 'a God who, in his act of incarnation, freely *identified himself with his own shit*, with the excremental Real that is man'. And this is precisely what God's love amounts to in a Christian point of view: 'love for the miserable excremental entity called "man"' (*PV* 187).

But only at the moment of utmost abjection and humiliation Christ truly became Christ, the 'ultimate *objet petit a*' (*OB* 140), the incarnation of the human excess as such, that excess which can never be contained within the symbolic order of exchange. (Cf. *PV* 97: 'It is only in his death on the Cross that Christ – up to that point a man who was a divine messenger – directly became God'.) Thus, precisely by becoming himself a piece of shit, God effected our redemption. For, as the ultimate *objet petit a*, Christ 'assume[d], contract[ed] onto himself, the excess ("Sin") which burdened the human race'. Žižek elaborates on this redemption as follows:

> By taking upon himself all the Sins and then, through
> his death, paying for them, Christ opens up the way
> for the redemption of humanity – however, by his
> death, people are not directly redeemed, but given the
> POSSIBILITY of redemption, of getting rid of the
> excess. This distinction is crucial: Christ does NOT do
> our work for us, he does not pay our debt, he "merely"
> GIVES US A CHANCE – with his death, he asserts
> OUR freedom and responsibility, i.e. he "merely" opens
> up the possibility, for us, to redeem ourselves through
> the "leap into faith", i.e. by way of choosing to "live in
> Christ" – in *imitatio Christi*, we REPEAT Christ's gesture
> of freely assuming the excess of Life, instead of projecting/
> displacing it onto some figure of the Other (*OB* 105).

Of course, this promising fragment, which concludes the second part of *On Belief*, raises the question of what Žižek means by 'freely assuming the excess of Life'. Unfortunately, he does not concretize this. Also the other expressions in the fragment just quoted above which seem to refer to what praxis is now expected from us – namely 'leap into faith', 'to live in Christ' and '*imitatio Christi*' remain vague and do not receive any further specification. Moreover, it is also not immediately clear what is precisely meant by 'projecting/displacing [the excess of Life] onto some figure of the Other', seemingly our usual way to deal with this excess. This sounds rather obscure, though from *The Puppet and the Dwarf*, we can conclude that 'life in Christ' has to do with 'the suspension of Otherness' (*PD* 138). Another clue is also to be found in *The Puppet and the Dwarf*. In it, Žižek speaks about God's own Pascalian wager:

> [B]y dying on the Cross, He made a risky gesture with no
> guaranteed final outcome, . . . .. Far from providing the
> conclusive dot on the i, the divine act stands, rather for the

openness of a New Beginning, and it is up to humanity to live up to it, to decide its meaning, to make something of it. . . . through the Event (of Christ), we are *formally* redeemed, subsumed under Redemption, and we have to engage in the difficult work of actualizing it (*PD* 136–37).

Translated into theological terms, this means, in Žižek's view, that we should not expect any divine help anymore. On the contrary, Žižek states, adopting an idea expressed by Etty Hillesum, it is we who must help God. Žižek further elaborates on this by referring to Hans Jonas, who expressed the view that creation implies divine self-limitation. Before creating, God had to contract himself in order to make room for creation (*PD* 137). A similar view was already expressed in *On Belief*, in which Žižek states that the existence of humankind is only possible thanks to God's self-limitation, his imperfection (*OB* 146).

## g. Christ as 'Vanishing Mediator': From God-the-Father to the Holy Spirit as Revolutionary Collective

When discussing the Christological ideas found in the recent work of Žižek, one should also point to a persistent Hegelian theme which appears in these books and which suggests that Žižek is, with regard to Christianity, actually in the first place a Hegelian before being a Lacanian. He adopts the basic scheme of Hegel's *Lectures on the Philosophy of Religion* according to which the God of Beyond dies on the cross and passes into the Holy Spirit *as* the community of believers. This basic idea is endorsed by Žižek in *Did Sombeody Say Totalitarianism?*, but it appears also in *The Fragile Absolute*, *On Belief* and *The Puppet and the Dwarf*. Actually, it forms the foundation of all his works on Christianity.

In *Did Somebody Say Totalitarianism?*, the Holy Spirit is designated as 'the figure of the reunification of God and humanity'. But in order for this reunification to take place, Christ, the mediator between God and humankind, has to disappear again: before Christ's death, the Holy Spirit cannot come. As long as Christ is still here, the unification of God and humankind remains limited to a singular individual. This is clarified by Žižek with the help of a syllogism. To reach the conclusion that 'humanity is fully united with God' starting from the premises 'Christ is God's Son, fully Divine' and 'Christ is man's son, fully human', the middle-term (Christ) has to be crossed out. Christ is a 'vanishing mediator'. This suggests that Christ is not a mediation between two entities that remain distinct and separate. For, in that case, the mediation would stop with Christ's death. In Christ, in contrast, both God and humankind are radically altered, transubstantiated (the use of this term is Žižek's):

> On the one hand, Christ is the vanishing mediator/
> medium through whose death God the Father himself
> 'passes into' the Holy Spirit; on the other hand, he is
> the vanishing mediator/medium through whose death
> the human community itself 'passes into' the new
> spiritual stage.

Thus, to conclude: Christ did not come into the world to open a direct communication line between humankind and a God that remains beyond and to whom he returns after his death (cf. *PV* 109–10). No, since Christ, '*there is no longer any transcendent God with whom to communicate*'. God has passed into the Holy Spirit *as* the (spirit of the) community of believers (*DSST* 50–51). Similar ideas are found in *On Belief*, where the Holy Spirit is described as 'the community of believers onto which the unfathomable aura of Christ passes once it is deprived of its bodily incarnation' (*OB* 91), and in *The Puppet and the Dwarf*, where Žižek states that the dead God-the-Father 'rises from the dead in the guise of the Holy Spirit' (*PD* 126).

But what about the character of the community which is the Holy Spirit? In *The Fragile Absolute*, Žižek characterizes it as a community of 'outcasts', of subjects who have 'uncoupled' themselves from the prevailing social order and are 'no longer rooted in a particular substance', but are 'redeemed of all particular links' (*FA* 158, 160). The same idea is found in *The Puppet and the Dwarf*, in which the Holy Spirit is described as

> a new collective [that is] held together ... by fidelity to a
> Cause, by the effort to draw a new line of separation that

runs "beyond Good and Evil," that is to say, that runs across and suspends the distinctions of the existing social body (*PD* 130).

To elaborate on this characterization of the community that is the Holy Spirit as a kind of revolutionary collective of individuals breaking away from the existing social body, we can turn to Žižek's discussion of the opposition between Christianity and paganism, as presented in *The Fragile Absolute*.

In *The Fragile Absolute*, Žižek describes the pagan universe as a 'Divine hierarchical order of cosmic Principles'. This view of the cosmos entails a particular understanding of what Good, Evil and Justice are. Good in the pagan cosmos is 'the global balance of Principles', a state in which opposites coincide and balance each other out (male/female, feeling/reason, contemplation/action, etc.). Evil, in contrast, is the excessive stress on one principle at the detriment of others. Justice, in this regard, amounts to re-establishing the global equilibrium. In a similar vein, the pagan view of society understands society as 'a congruent edifice in which each member has its own place'. The Indian caste system is the ultimate example of this. In such a view of society, the individual is good when it acts in accordance with the place it occupies in the ordered Whole of the social body. An individual is evil, in contrast, when it is no longer content with that place and begins to revolt against the Whole by refusing to act in accordance with the place it occupies in the Whole.

Christianity, however, broke with this pagan understanding of cosmos and society by stressing the immediate participation of each individual to the universal dimension: regardless of the place an individual occupies in the Whole of the social edifice, it has direct access to the Holy Spirit (*FA* 119–20). According to Žižek, this is stressed by Jesus by addressing the dregs of society (prostitutes, tax-collectors, lepers . . .) as the privileged members of the group he gathers around him (*FA* 123). It is also the meaning of the shocking words in Lk. 14.26, where Jesus says that 'Whoever comes to me and does not hate father and mother, wife and children, brothers and sisters, yes, and even life itself, cannot be my disciple'. In Žižek's view, the family relations mentioned in this verse stand 'for the entire socio-symbolic network, for any particular ethnic "substance" that determines our place in the global Order of Things'. The hatred requested here by Jesus is therefore a call to cut ourselves loose from 'the organic community into which we were born'. It is a call to 'unplug', to 'uncouple' from the Whole. This makes clear that the Christ-Event is about 'separation' ('drawing the line', 'clinging to an element that disturbs the balance of All'), about 'the violent intrusion of Difference that precisely *throws the balanced circuit of the universe off the rails*' (*FA* 120–21). In this regard, one should also understand statements such as the one in which Jesus tells us to offer the other cheek. These are not at all about 'stupid masochism', but about breaking the pagan logic of revenge as the way to re-establish the disturbed equilibrium (*FA* 125). For the same reason it is 'profoundly anti-Christian' to compare Christ's death on the cross with the seasonal death and rebirth of many pagan gods. Christ's death is not at all of that kind, but is on the contrary a break with this logic. Reducing Christ's death to the pagan scheme amounts therefore to cancelling 'the subversive core of Christianity' (*FA* 118–19).

From the point of view of paganism, striving for equilibrium, the Christ-Event, resulting in separation and difference, can, of course, only appear as the ultimate Evil. It may not come as a surprise then that in the universe of George Lucas's *Star Wars*-series, which is the pagan universe of New Age, Darth Vader, the embodiment of pure Evil, appears with Christological features. (In this regard, Žižek refers to the fact that in *Star Wars I: The Phantom Menace*, the mother of Anakin Skywalker – who would only later turn into Darth Vader – suggests that the boy, like Jesus, was conceived without the intervention of a father.) That the context of *Star Wars* is indeed the one of (neo)paganism can also be derived from the fact that initially Anakin was thought to be a saviour who would *restore the balance* of the Force, a kind of power which permeates in *Star Wars* the entire universe. As a result, the entire *Star Wars*-series circles, in Žižek's view, around one pivotal question, namely the one of the origins of Evil: '*[H]ow did Darth Vader become Darth Vader*, that is, how did Anakin Skywalker, this sweet boy, turn into the monstrous instrument of cosmic Evil?' (*FA* 121–22). This question is elaborated upon by Žižek in *The Parallax View*. In it, he refers to Lucas's explanation of this transition, who draws in this regard a parallel between the personal level (the transition from Anakin into Darth Vader) and the political level (the transition from the 'good', democratic Republic into the 'bad', dictatorial Empire). The crucial point is that the Republic has not been conquered by the Empire, but turned itself into the Empire as a result of the way the former combated its enemies. (In this respect, Žižek makes a comparison with the USA and its war on terror: '[T]he bad Empire is not out there; it emerges through the very way we, the "good guys," fight the bad Empire, the enemy out there – in today's "war on terror," the problem is what this war will turn the USA into'.) However, according to Žižek, the failure of the *Star Wars*-series is precisely that Lucas has not succeeded in drawing the parallel between the personal and the political level he himself proposed. While on the political level, the transition from the Republic to the Empire indeed suggests that Evil can be the outcome of the Good (combating terrorists turns us in evil guys as well), this suggestion is completely absent from the transition of Anakin to Darth Vader. Instead of presenting Anakin as becoming Darth Vader as a result of his excessive attachment to do Good for his beloved ones (and in particular for his love, Amidala), he is merely depicted as 'an indecisive warrior who is gradually sliding into evil by giving way to the temptation of Power'. In this way, the transition from Anakin to Darth Vader is merely an example of a 'pop-Buddhist cliché'. To put it in the words of Lucas himself, quoted by Žižek:

> [Anakin] turns into Darth Vader because he gets attached to things. He can't let go of his mother; he can't let go of his girlfriend. He can't let go of things. It makes you greedy. And when you're greedy, you are on the path to the dark side, because you fear you're going to lose things (*PV* 100–01).

In contrast to this pagan wisdom, however, which pleads for detachment and indifference, harmony and balance, Christianity stresses love. The difference between (neo)paganism/New Age and Christianity is therefore the difference between 'Buddhist (or Hindu, for that matter) all-encompassing Compassion' and 'Christian *intolerant, violent* Love' (*PV* 282). Indeed, *true* Christian love is always violent because it is an 'excessive care for the beloved, a "biased" commitment which disturbs the balance of the Whole' (*PV* 103), 'a violent passion to introduce a Difference, a gap in the order of Being, to privilege and elevate some object at the expense of others' (*PV* 282). Or, to put it still differently, 'The choice of love itself is already violent, as it tears an object out of its context and elevates it to the [dignity of the] Thing.'[32] So, to return to Darth Vader: rather than denouncing him as an embodiment of pure evil, we should hail him as 'a *good* figure' who makes clear that ethical commitment has a diabolical foundation, the '"excessive" care and attachment, our readiness to break the balance of the ordinary flow of life, and to put everything at stake for the Cause to which we adhere' (*PV* 103). In this regard, moreover, we should also conclude that Christ himself is 'the ultimate diabolic figure', who has come to tear apart the existing social body (*diabolos* meaning, as Žižek notes, the one who separates, who tears 'apart the One into Two'). In this regard, Žižek also speaks about Christ bringing 'the sword, not peace' (*PV* 99). This is of course a reference to Mt. 10.34–39, where Jesus says the following:

> Do not think that I have come to bring peace to
> the earth; I have not come to bring peace, but a sword.
> For I have come to set a man against his father, and a
> daughter against her mother, and a daughter-in-law
> against her mother-in-law; and one's foes will be
> members of one's own household. Whoever loves father
> or mother more than me is not worthy of me; and
> whoever loves son or daughter more than me is not
> worthy of me; and whoever does not take up the cross
> and follow me is not worthy of me. Those who find
> their life will lose it, and those who lose their life for
> my sake will find it.

---

[32] *Cyprano's Journal Online/Revenge of Global Finance By Slavoj Žižek*, http://www.bestcyrano.org/slavojZizekRevengeofFinance207.htm (access: 30/04/2007).

It is only thanks to this act of separation, finally, that the gathering (*symbolos* as opposite of *diabolos*) of an alternative community, the collective that is the Holy Spirit, becomes possible (*PV* 99).

In *The Fragile Absolute* Žižek even goes a step further by stating that Christian love finds its culmination point in the *hatred of 'the beloved* out of love and in love', an idea which he adopts from Kierkegaard. This hatred 'out of love and in love' should of course be understood correctly. What we should hate is the beloved insofar as s/he is part of the symbolic order (his or her substance) and this in name of my love for her/him as a unique person, a '*singular point of subjectivity*' (*FA* 127).[33] This entails that there is a fundamental distinction between the *content of a subject* (its substance) and the *subject as such*. The content of the subject is our identity, which comes into being as the result of our identification with signifiers and images. The subject as such, however, is an empty space in which these signifiers and images appear. As a result, it is important to distinguish between a beloved one as substance (the beloved as this particular human being with this or that particular character and these particular features) and a beloved one as subject as such (the beloved as a 'singular point of subjectivity' irreducible to a set of particular features). Moreover, according to Žižek in *The Fragile Absolute*, 'the Christian work of compassionate love' precisely enables us to make the transition from the neighbour as 'a disturbing foreign body' (a sleazy and repulsive substance) to the neighbour as 'a subject, with its crushed dreams and desires'. Love is thus always 'the *work* of love', 'the hard and arduous work of repeated "uncoupling" in which, again and again, we have to disengage ourselves from the inertia that constrains us to identify with the particular order we were born into'. This makes clear that Christian uncoupling can not at all be compared with the pagan view that one should get involved in the hurly-burly of the world, but while keeping peace of mind.

---

[33] We should understand Žižek correctly, however. He is *not* endorsing the standard 'humanist' cliché according to which behind the masks people wear and the roles they are playing, there is always a warm and loving human being which calls for our comprehension and compassion (*FA* 126). As we shall see in what follows, Christian is precisely *not* concerned with this, but with the other as empty point of pure singularity.

Christian unplugging is not contemplation, but the creation of a new collective (*FA* 128–30).

All this brings us to the 'good news' of Christianity. By tearing apart the existent social edifice, Christ has taught us that we are more than a substance. We are also a subject which is always more that every particular filling-in of it. Therefore, we are *not* condemned to remain locked up in our primary community, the community in which we were by chance born. Conversion is possible: a temporal act *can* change eternity itself (*FA* 97). Or, as Žižek puts it: a new beginning is possible. We can clean the slate and start all over again from scratch (*FA* 127). In *On Belief*, this new beginning is elaborated upon with the help of Schelling's depiction of a 'primordial decision-differentiation (*Entscheidung*)'. Žižek describes this as 'the unconscious atemporal deed by means of which the subject chooses his/her eternal character which, afterwards, within his/her conscious-temporal life, is experienced as the inexorable necessity, as "the way s/he always was"'. Žižek also translates this primordial choice in psychoanalytic terms as the fundamental fantasy, which is 'the basic frame/matrix which provides the coordinates of the subject's entire universe of meaning' and of which Žižek writes that 'although I am never outside it, although this fantasy is always-already here, and I am always-already thrown into it, I have to presuppose myself as the one who posited it'. This brings Žižek to the following formulation of the 'good news' brought by Christ:

> [T]he miracle of faith is that it IS possible to traverse the fantasy, to undo this founding decision, to start one's life all over again, from the zero point – in short, *to change Eternity itself* (*what we "always-already are"*). Ultimately, the "rebirth" of which Christianity speaks (when one joins the community of believers, one is born again) is the name for such a new Beginning. Again the pagan and/or Gnostic Wisdom which celebrates the (re)discovery of one's true Self – the return to it, the realization of its potentials or whatsoever – Christianity calls upon us to thoroughly reinvent ourselves. Kierkegaard was right: the ultimate choice is the one between the Socratic recollection and the Christian repetition: Christianity

enjoins us to REPEAT the founding gesture of the primordial choice. . . . And THIS Christian legacy, often obfuscated, is today more precious than ever (*OB* 147–48).

This, of course, raises the question of how somebody can give up his or her substance to become a subject. In *The Fragile Absolute*, Žižek suggests that this asks for 'a radical gesture of "striking at oneself"' (*FA* 150). This brings us to the distinction between traditional, pre-modern and modern, ethical sacrifice. In the first case, somebody is prepared to give up everything for the Thing which matters most to him/her (*FA* 154). Examples of this are Abraham (who is prepared to sacrifice even his only son to his God) and Antigone (who is willing to give up everything, even her very life, in order to have her brother buried). The Thing itself, however, is *not* given up. The properly modern ethical act precisely consists in also sacrificing the Thing and this out of love, out of fidelity to the Thing (*FA* 154). An example of this is to be found in Toni Morrison's *Beloved* in which the heroine, Sethe, escapes from slavery with her four children and, when caught, kills her eldest daughter and threatens to kill her other children in order to spare them a life in slavery. According to Žižek, the crucial point is that we are here not at all dealing with some primitive deed of mere brutality. On the contrary, Sethe killed her children out of love. Such a monstrous act of giving up of what is most precious to us out of love and fidelity to the precious Thing, is what is, in Žižek's view, the only true ethical act (*FA* 152–53, 154).

In *On Belief* Žižek speaks, in a similar vein, about 'the religious suspension of the ethical'. In this regard, he refers to Evelyn Waugh's *Brideshead Revisited*, in which we get Julia sacrificing everything, including her marriage and reputation, for her love for Ryder and then continuing by also giving up Ryder himself. Yet, here the question should be raised of whether the acts of Sethe in *Beloved* and Julia in *Brideshead Revisited* are of the same kind. For, though both in *The Fragile Absolute* and *On Belief*, Žižek distinguishes between ordinary sacrifice (sacrifice *for* the Thing) and a truer kind of sacrifice (sacrifice *of* the Thing), there nevertheless seems to be an important shift of emphasis between both books. While in *The Fragile Absolute*, the stress is on giving up the

Thing out of love for the Thing, in *On Belief*, the stress is on renouncing that what is most precious for us *for nothing* (cf. *OB* 77, where *self*-sacrifice for a Thing is opposed to *self*-sacrifice for *nothing*, the former being merely 'moral' while the latter is 'properly ethical'; see also p. 67, where the opposition is between sacrifice and renunciation). In this regard, however, the example of Julia from *Brideshead Revisited* turns out to be dubious. For, as Žižek notes, Julia drops the man for which she has ruined her marriage and reputation 'as part of what she ironically refers to as her "private deal" with God': the only way to retain a small chance to receive God's mercy is by choosing for a promiscuous life with numerous affairs instead of choosing to marry Ryder because 'there should be no competition between supreme goods' and her love for Ryder should therefore not interfere with her dedication to God (*OB* 149–50). Is this not a return to the good old logic of sacrificing everything for the Thing which is most precious to us and which in the case of Julia turns out to be ultimately God instead of Ryder? Or is this not the case? How can we understand that Julia sacrifices Ryder *for nothing*? Of course, she is not giving him up to receive something in return in the here and now (such as this-worldly happiness: marrying Ryder, her true love, would make her much happier than the numerous short-term affairs she will engage in after she has dropped him). From, the standpoint of 'a "rational" subject of utilitarianism' (see above), Julia's act of giving up Ryder is indeed completely useless, a 'purely negative gesture of meaningless sacrifice' (*OB* 150). But is Julia not doing it for a higher goal, namely receiving God's mercy?

So, what about the likeness and difference between Sethe and Julia? In both cases we get an act of giving up of the most precious Thing (Sethe's children, Julia's true love). In the case of Seth, however, the act of hitting oneself is motivated by love for the object which is given up and this turns Seth, according to Žižek, into a true ethical figure. Had Julia been like Seth, she would also have given Ryder up but then out of love for him. Maybe she would even have killed him out of love and fidelity. (Cf. Kierkegaard's hatred of the beloved in love and out of love: in order to love my beloved as singular point of subjectivity I have to get rid off the beloved's substance and what better way to do this than killing

# Slavoj Žižek

him/her in order to reduce him/her to nothing but a name, an empty signifier to which I can attach myself?) Julia, however, motivates her act of sacrifice by speaking about a private deal with God. Why invoking God here? What is the meaning of God here? (That Žižek speaks about God as 'ultimately the name for the purely negative gesture of meaningless sacrifice, of giving up what matters most to us' [OB 150] does not do much to clarify things.) But that Žižek indeed suggests a difference between Sethe and Julia seems to have to be derived from the fact that, while Sethe is designated as truly ethical, Julia is an example of the religious suspension of the ethical. This seems to indicate that Julia is ultimately even more radical than Sethe.

Žižek leaves his readers with many questions: (1) The relation between the sacrifice *of* the Thing *out of love* (cf. *The Fragile Absolute*) and *self*-sacrifice *for nothing* (cf. *On Belief*) remains unclear. Are they to be identified? (If yes: but how?) Or are they two different ways to escape from the logic of ordinary sacrifice (sacrifice *for* the Thing), two different ways in which we can give up the Thing, two different figures of a truly ethical act? (2) The precise relation between renunciation (self-sacrifice for nothing) as truly ethical act (according to *OB* 77) and the religious suspension of the ethical of which Žižek speaks towards the end of *On Belief* also remains in the dark. Are they the same? But how can a truly ethical act and a religious suspension of the ethical coincide? Or is Žižek suggesting that one only acts truly ethical if one suspends the ethical? (3) And what about the meaning of the word 'ethical' as used by Žižek? Is it maybe used equivocally, referring simultaneously towards everyday morality and truly ethical acts of breaking with that morality, of moving beyond good and evil in the everyday sense? Indeed, both Sethe and Julia break with everyday morality (see also *OB* 150, where Žižek opposes everyday morality and faith understood as unconditional engagement – but is this engagement to be characterized as ethical or not?). (4) Things are even complicated further when it becomes clear that both the sacrifice of the Thing out of love for the Thing (cf. *The Fragile Absolute*) and the self-sacrifice for nothing (cf. *On Belief*) are linked to the Crucifixion. In *The Fragile Absolute*, Žižek concludes that 'the ultimate example of such a gesture of "shooting at oneself", renouncing what is most precious to oneself,

[is] again provided by Christianity itself, by the Crucifixion' (*FA* 157). In *On Belief*, he writes that 'this "empty" sacrifice is the Christian gesture par excellence: it is only against the background of this empty gesture that one can begin to appreciate the uniqueness of the figure of Christ' (*OB* 79). But how should we understand these statements in light of all what has been said up till now? In which way is the Crucifixion as sacrifice of the Thing out of love for the Thing/self-sacrifice for nothing to be linked with the Crucifixion as the moment in which Christ becomes the ultimate *objet petit a* by freely assuming the excess of Life? What is the Thing which is given up by Christ on the cross? Probably the Divine Thing. But how should we understand that this is done out of love for this Divine Thing (since Christ *is* God is he then merely giving up himself and acting out of a strange kind of *self*-love)? And in which way sacrifices Christ himself *for nothing* (though he of course becomes *nothing* but a piece of shit on the cross)?

What is clear however, is that the religious suspension of ethics asks for a leap into faith, with faith being understood as 'an unconditional subjective engagement' which implies suspending our substance (*OB* 151). Such an engagement is what Žižek finds in both Sethe and Julia. It is also what is, in his view, at stake in Christianity. According to Žižek in the last lines of *On Belief*, Christianity's idea of being born again in faith offers us precisely 'the first full fledged formulation of such an unconditional subjective engagement on account of which we are ready to suspend the very . . . substance of our being' (*OB* 151). This, however, brings us to a last series of questions: How can we choose to live like Christ, to imitate and repeat him? How can we leap into faith? Can we choose for the kind of unconditional engagement found in Sethe and Julia (which, after all, are merely figures from novels)? Can we voluntarily become such a 'singular point of subjectivity' Žižek is talking about? These questions in particular make clear that Žižek leaves his readers with a strong feeling of dissatisfaction. For, though he offers us fascinating analyses, the question unavoidably pops up of how these fascinating analyses can be made fruitful for practice in daily life. With regard to this very pressing questions, however, Žižek seems (yet) to remain silent.

# 3. Evaluation

In the concluding section of this chapter we first evaluate Žižek's claim that God's transcendence ends with the incarnation. Afterwards, we compare Žižek with Vattimo as well as with Girard.

## a. The End of God's Transcendence?

In order to evaluate Žižek's claim that God's transcendence ends with the incarnation, we shall discuss the way Žižek deals with human self-transcendence and raise the question of whether his work leaves any room for some form of superior transcendence, a transcendence which cannot be reduced to human activity. Human self-transcendence refers to the fact that human beings possess the power to surpass themselves. They can overcome themselves and become what they were not yet. In this regard, Dutch theologian Tjeu van Knippenberg speaks about 'the ability to human beings to go beyond themselves, to come to the realization that they are not limited to themselves and do not belong to themselves'.[34] This self-surpassing power can be linked with the movement of desire as we have described it above while discussing Žižek. As we have also indicated then, this movement of desire underlies the ever accelerating pace of human cultural evolution. And as has also already been seen above, Žižek claims the movement of desire to be a secondary phenomenon, considering it as a way to deal with the, much more fundamental, appearance of the drive, the stubborn attachment characterizing the human being, the excess of freedom that can never again be integrated into smooth, biological life. Desire comes into being when the invention/intervention of the Law places the impossible object of the drive into an inaccessible Beyond as a forbidden Thing. In this way, Žižek seems to suggest a kind of Feuerbachian theory of projection; his theory of desire, as we have outlined it in the previous section, seems to imply that the superior transcendence of

---

[34] Tjeu van Knippenberg, 'Transcendence and Personal History/Life Stories', *The Human Image of God* (Festschrift Johannes A. van der Ven; ed. Hans-Georg Ziebert *et al.*; Leiden, Boston, MA, and Köln: Brill, 2001) pp. 263–84 (263).

the Divine Thing is the result of the projection of the impossibility inherent in human existence into an inaccessible Beyond. Maybe, this is what Žižek means when he speaks in the final paragraph of the second part of *On Belief* about 'projecting/displacing [the excess of Life] onto some figure of the Other'. With his plea for a transition from the Thing to the *objet petit a*, and from tragic desire to love/drive, Žižek seems to be placing himself in the line of the Left Hegelians; for instance, in the line of Feuerbach's critique of religion as projection and Marx's critique of religion as alienation. The main difference between Žižek and these predecessors, however, is that, for Žižek, Christianity is no longer accused, but is, on the contrary, adopted as an important tool in his critical endeavours.

As outlined by Jason Glynos in his discussion of Žižek's anticapitalism, there is, according to Žižek, a direct link between the subject of desire, moving from the one substitute for the impossible/forbidden Thing to the next, and the subject of capitalism, consuming one commodity after the other.[35] Thus, as Žižek expects, breaking away from the logic of desire will enable a break with capitalism. And since Christianity offers us, at least according to Žižek, the eminent example of such a break with the logic of desire, Žižek considers it as a main source for the anti-capitalist struggle. Indeed, in order to think the revolutionary subject Žižek falls back on Christianity. Initially – for instance in *The Sublime Object of Ideology* (1989) – Žižek merely stated that a revolutionary praxis asks for a moment of decision which can be compared with

---

[35] Jason Glynos, 'Symptoms of a Decline in Symbolic Faith, or, Žižek's Anticapitalism', *Paragraph* 24/2 (2001), pp. 78–110 (87) (emphasis added):

> The suggestion here is that Lacan's logic of desire and the logic of capitalism share a deep homology in structuring contemporary subjectivity. This is because, just as the subject of capitalism is empty, so too is the subject of desire. In both case, the logics are purely formal and independent of the particular concrete contexts wherein they function. The discourse of *capitalism can only have as its main objective the failure to satisfy desire, thereby keeping desire alive, sustaining an insatiable desire for new products, new commodities*, thereby leading to a kind of 'fetishism of the new' whose consequence is the ever-expanding frontiers of capitalist market relations.

the 'leap of faith' and he used the example of the famous Pascalian wager to illustrate this point (*SOI* 38–40). Yet, in his more recent work (from the 1999 *The Ticklish Subject* onwards), the *content* of Christianity has increasingly become a central concern for Žižek. As pointed out by Michael Moriarty in his discussion of Žižek's use of religion, it is as if without theological notions, Žižek is not (or no longer) able to analyse the contemporary situation of the subject.[36] Thus, where initially Žižek only saw an analogy between the believer and the revolutionary subject, as being two species of the same genus, in his more recent work he analyses the latter in terms of the former.[37] It may not come as a surprise then that, in the introduction to *The Fragile Absolute*, Žižek pleads for an alliance between Christianity and Marxism (*FA* 2). In the introduction to *The Puppet and the Dwarf*, he is even more explicit when he claims that 'the subversive kernel of Christianity ... is accessible *only* to a materialist approach – and vice versa: to become a true dialectical materialist, one should go through the Christian experience' (*PD* 6).

Thus, Christian faith seems to be used by Žižek as a tool to think the possibility of an anti-capitalist praxis. For Žižek, we will be able to break away from the logic of capitalism by giving up the logic of tragic desire and re-entering the domain of the drive and of love. It has become clear, however, that this transition from desire to drive implies a complete abandonment of any superior transcendence. Indeed, all superior transcendences – be it the superior transcendence of the Judeo-Christian tradition or its many immanent substitutes (be it an ultimate principle of reality or a utopia) – seem to be condemned as being as many appearances of the Thing preserving the logic of desire and, therefore,

[36] Michael Moriarty, 'Žižek, Religion and Ideology', *Paragraph* 24/2 (2001), pp. 125–39 (129): 'The situation is slightly different in Žižek's more recent work. For here we find explicitly theological concepts being invoked to theorize the condition of the subject, as if without them the modern predicament of choice could not be analysed.'

[37] Moriarty, 'Žižek, Religion and Ideology', pp. 130–31: '[I]t is clear that the analogy of proletarian and religious commitment is not quite the same as in the earlier work. The former is no longer interpreted merely as resembling the latter, but by means of concepts drawn from the latter.'

modern capitalism. As a result, re-entering the domain of the drive – being, to use the way Žižek had already put it in his 1997 *The Plague of Fantasies*, 'the domain of the closed circular palpitation which finds satisfaction in endlessly repeating the same failed gesture' – cannot but imply 'a radical ontological closure'. Leaving the domain of tragic desire requires that we give up the belief 'that there is some radical Otherness which makes our universe incomplete'. Or to put it differently, entering the domain of the drive means renouncing 'every opening, every belief in the messianic Otherness'.[38] In this way, Žižek is indeed ending up with a complete denial of transcendence.

Žižek's claim that we have to abandon every form of superior transcendence in order to break with capitalism raises two major questions. (1) On the one hand, there is, of course, the question whether Žižek is not merely (mis)using Christianity in function of his own critical endeavours and maybe we may even take the risk here of speaking about Žižek using Christianity, interpreted along Lacanian and Hegelian lines, as the *ancilla* of his Marxist aspirations. (2) On the other hand, there is also the question whether the end of superior transcendences – including utopias such as 'the Kingdom of God' or 'the classless society' – is not precisely advancing capitalism instead of combating it. Is the absence of alternatives for the current capitalist status quo not contributing to the post-revolutionary climate characterizing contemporary Western culture? Moreover, in what way can the 'subject of drive' – locked up as it is in its eternal, circular movement – ever become the basic unit of a new revolutionary movement? And is, in contrast, the problem of capitalism not, instead of being a problem of desire as such, rather a problem of *perverted* desire, of desire disconnected from a superiorly transcendent aim? Are we, therefore, not in need of a truly superior transcendence in order to heal our desire and our world from the onslaught of capitalism?

[38] Slavoj Žižek, *The Plague of Fantasies* (Wo es war; London and New York, NY:Verso, 1997) pp. 30–31.

Slavoj Žižek

## b. Žižek and Vattimo: The Persistence of Hegelian Christology and the Problem of Supercessionism

Both Žižek and Vattimo identify the incarnation as the moment at which God's transcendence ends: the God of Beyond, the Eternal Father, dies and is irrevocably lost. Žižek is quite explicit about the source of this idea: he attributes it to Hegel who is, as we have seen, one of his major sources of inspiration. Vattimo, in contrast, couches this view in Heideggerian terminology, but the fact that he is, as we have outlined in Chapter 1 above, tributary to Altizer's 'God is dead'-theology, of which Hegel is one of the major sources, suggests that Vattimo is also more under the spell of Hegel than he is willing to admit. This point has recently been made by Anthony Sciglitano in a contribution to *Modern Theology*. In his article, Sciglitano detects seven points in which Vattimo is influenced by Hegelian Christology:

> (1) the Trinity is de-personalized; (2) the divine-world relation is given a modalistic and ultimately monistic reading; (3) Passibility is radical and history becomes constitutive, or stronger, determinative, of divine being; (4) Scriptural revelation is overcome by a "spiritual sense" reading that envisions a reconciliation between divine being and the being of the world, thus asserting some form of identity; (5) Jesus' historical existence becomes religiously insignificant; (6) Resurrection does not lead to exaltation and end kenosis, and does not apply to Jesus as an individual, but rather continues kenosis as a general diffusion of divine Being into the secular or as the secular; (7) Divine will, election, missions are excised from theological reflection.[39]

This suggests that, while Vattimo and Žižek may be very different with regard to the content of their Christological reflections (the former offering a Christology which (mis)reads Girard through Heidegger, the latter a Christology which develops a basic idea

---

[39] Sciglitano, 'Contesting the World and the Divine', p. 538.

139

from Hegel with the help of Lacanian terminology), they are actually both continuations of Hegelian Christology. In postmodern philosophical Christological reflections, the ghost of Hegel turns out to be still alive.

In Chapter 1, we mentioned that Vattimo's Christology appears to be supercessionist. According to John Caputo, this supercessionism is a result of Vattimo's affinity with 'God is dead'-theology and its scheme, which it shares with and adopts from Hegel, of a 'transition from transcendence to immanence, from alienation and estrangement to homecoming, from God as a distant and severe Father to God first as Son and sibling and then as the spirit of love'. In this master narrative, however, Caputo adds, 'Somebody has to play the bad guy' and this 'bad guy' is invariably 'the religion of the Father' or Judaism.[40] The fact that Žižek also adopts the Hegelian scheme of a transition from transcendence to immanence suggests that the problem of supercessionism will also be present in his work. The relation of Žižek towards Judaism is indeed ambiguous. On the one hand, Žižek states that God-the-Father dies on the cross and becomes the Holy Spirit *as* the community of believers. God as the wholly other Thing dies and becomes barely nothing. This transition is explicitly linked by Žižek with the one from Judaism to Christianity and this suggests that in Žižek's view the Jewish manner of relating to God is ruled out now that Christ has come. On the other hand, Žižek also states that Christianity needs Judaism to remind itself of the otherness of the Divine Thing (*OB* 142). This remark, however, is difficult to reconcile with the rest of Žižek's Christological reflections as we have outlined them in the present chapter. With regard to Islam, by the way, it has to be noticed that Islam is almost completely absent from Žižek's works on religion. His most important reference to it is in a footnote in *On Belief*, in which he states that Islam, in its attempt to synthesize Judaism and Christianity, 'ends up with the worst of both worlds' (*OB* 162 [n.40]). Žižek's view of Buddhism, finally, has become more negative in the past few years. While in *The Fragile Absolute*, he considered also Buddhism as offering an immediate participation of each

---

[40] Caputo and Vattimo, *After the Death of God*, pp. 79–80.

individual to the universal dimension and, therefore, as a disturbance of the hierarchical order of the pagan universe (*FA* 120, 123), the first chapter of *The Puppet and the Dwarf* offers a polemic against Buddhism, in particular against Zen (*PD* 26–33). In it, Žižek opposes Christian love to Buddhist and Hindu compassion, an opposition which also returns, as we have seen, in *The Parallax View*.

## c. Girard vs. Žižek: Shared Intuitions, Divergent Conclusion

There are clearly important points of agreement between Girard's 'violence of the sacred' and Žižek's 'excess of life':

1. Both Girard and Žižek trace the origins of human culture back to the moment when the human animal was contaminated by something, causing that animal to leave the domain of smooth, spontaneous biological life and to become truly human.
2. This something, which makes us human, is, according to both thinkers, a 'too much', an excess: an excess of violence (in the case of Girard) or an excessive – and for this reason also violent – attachment to a Thing (in the case of Žižek).
3. This excess, though it is what makes us human, is also what threatens us the most. As Girard mentions, violence can result in complete destruction of human society and, as Žižek makes clear, the stubborn attachment to a Thing can lead to an addiction at the cost of our own health, well-being or even life (which is, by the way, the reason why Freud introduced his concept of the 'death drive').
4. Furthermore, in both cases, culture (Girard's sacrificial order, Žižek's Law of culture) aims at restricting and controlling this 'too much'; without, however, ever completely succeeding in that aim. A return to smooth and spontaneous, biological life is impossible. Or, to put it in the metaphor of Genesis 3, the way back to Paradise has been blocked by 'the cherubim, and a flaming sword which turns every way' (Gn. 3.24).

It is against this background that both Girard and Žižek interpret the incarnation of Christ:

5. Both authors offer an alternative interpretation of 'sin': sin is the excess by which the human being is contaminated.
6. Moreover, they both adopt the traditional view that Christ was without sin (without violence, without excess).
7. But precisely in this way, by being without excess himself, Christ was able to redeem humankind of its 'too much', either by showing it the way out of violence (as Girard states) or by showing that we should 'repeat Christ's gesture of freely assuming the excess of Life' (as Žižek puts it).

In this way, both authors reject the traditional view according to which Christ was the sacrifice needed to satisfy God's honour offended by human sin.

Moreover, as outlined by Žižek, it is not a matter of merely substituting an old, incorrect view (the sacrificial, legalistic one) for a newer, correct one (one which would no longer be sacrificial nor legalistic). The point is precisely that, within the horizon in which Christ's death on the cross took place, this event could not have been read differently than in the 'wrong' way – thus, in the legalistic way, as being a sacrifice. Christ's death can only become the access to something completely New by simultaneously being the absolute culmination point of the Old. So, it is precisely by becoming the ultimate sacrifice that Christ breaches the sacrificial order and installs 'a life which needs no sacrifice' anymore. For, after Christ's Crucifixion, every further sacrifice has become useless because, in Christ, God sacrificed Himself to Himself and, in this way, the highest sacrifice possible has already been brought.[41]

It is also important, however, to point to *the major difference between Žižek and Girard*. Žižek claims that the incarnation of Christ should be understood as the complete abolishment of God's transcendence. For, God is just the excess of Life projected 'onto some figure of the Other', Christ frees us from this Divine Thing and this liberation must lead to the abolishment of all (superior) transcendences. For Girard, in contrast, Christ reveals the true character of the truly superior transcendence: the truly

[41] Žižek, *The Puppet and the Dwarf*, p. 81 and p. 103.

transcendent reality is not violent but loving. As Girard claims, Christ liberates us from our excessive violence, but he could only do so by being completely without violence himself and, thus, by truly transcending our violence. So, in contrast to Žižek, Girard seems to leave room for transcendence. Therefore, we may conclude by expressing the expectation that, both for the struggle against capitalism and for Christianity, the work of Girard seems to be, at least at first sight, more promising than that of Žižek.

# General Conclusion

In the preceding pages, we have investigated the Christological reflections of three contemporary thinkers whose work does not have any institutional links with the Church or theology. Vattimo was a fervent Catholic during his youth, but later distanced himself from the Church, only returning to a weak version of Christianity in the 1990s. Girard began his intellectual career as an agnostic and only turned to Christianity (and to Catholicism in particular) as a result of his research as a literary critic and anthropologist. Žižek designates himself as a Paulinian materialist. As we have announced in the Introduction, we have approached the work of Vattimo, Girard and Žižek with the help of a double focus: the relation between transcendence and the event of the incarnation on the one hand and the topic of the uniqueness of Christianity on the other. With regard to the topic of transcendence, we have found that Vattimo and Žižek do not leave room for God's transcendence, a fact which we have attributed to the impact of Hegel's Christology (which is explicit in the case of Žižek and remains unspoken in that of Vattimo), while the work of Girard points us towards a transcendence of love which is even more transcendent than the humanly created transcendence of violence. We have already discussed this in Chapter 2 (subsection 3.a) and Chapter 3 (section 3) and will not return to it here. With regard to the other thread of this book, the question of the uniqueness of Christianity, we have found that all three of the thinkers who have been discussed defend this uniqueness, though in different ways. Vattimo follows the strategy used by 'God is dead'-theologian Altizer (and late-modern theology in general) and identifies secularization as the realization of the essence of Christianity. In Vattimo's view, the uniqueness of Christianity consists in the fact that it has ultimately a non-religious destiny: it is the religion in which humankind breaks free from religion and leaves the domain of the sacral to enter the domain of the secular. In a similar vein, Girard links religion to the violent origins of human culture and opposes Christianity to religion by claiming that in Christ these violent origins have been irrevocably revealed. In contrast to Vattimo, however, who seems to be offering a Christian legitimization for the end of Christianity and whose post-modern Christology does not seem able to cope with the current situation of *ressentiment*, global capitalism and universal violence, Girard offers us a way to accept modernity *critically*: modernity is the outcome of the impact of the Biblical message of love, but it is its *unfinished* impact. Žižek formulates his view on the uniqueness of Christianity in his Lacanian idiom. Christianity makes the transition from God as 'Wholly Other Thing' to God as 'Barely Nothing', from the domain of tragic desire to the one of drive and love. Love is moreover a major topic in the Christological reflections of all three thinkers discussed in the present volume. According to Vattimo, love (or caritas) is the core of the Biblical message and the only limit to the process of secularization initiated by the incarnation; Girard opposes the transcendence of love revealed by Christ to the humanly created violent transcendence; and Žižek characterizes Christianity as the religion of love. The meaning of this love, however, seems to be quite different for the different thinkers. Vattimo's caritas turns out to be a soft friendliness, the kind of tolerance of live and let live which is *bon ton* in many multiculturalist and liberal circles. Girard's love is an absolute and unconditional non-violence, which is subversive for the current order because that order is precisely based on violence. In Žižek's view, Christian love is not at all soft but, on the contrary, violent. It is the violent attachment to a particular person or cause, resulting in a break with the organic community in which we were born and the establishment of a new collective.

The main problem with the three defences of the uniqueness of Christianity offered by the three contemporary thinkers discussed in this book turns out to be the problem of supercessionism and, more in general, their view on the relation between Christianity and the non-Christian world religions. We have already seen that this is the case for both Vattimo and Žižek. But also the work of Girard raises this problem. Though Girard explicitly defends the continuity between the Old and the New Testament – it is the same inspiration which is active in both (*TH* 175–76) –, the question remains of what room there is left

for Judaism after Christ has fully and irrevocably revealed the violent origins of human culture, a revelation partly begun but not
completed by the Hebrew Scriptures. For Girard's view on Islam,
we can refer to an interview with the French newspaper *Le Monde*
which was published in 2001 in the wake of September 11. In that
interview, Girard states that also the Islamic tradition has pro-
phetic insights into the mechanisms of mimesis and violence, but
it lacks the most essential element, namely the cross. As a result,
Islam's concern for the innocent victim turns in an attempt to
rehabilitate the victim in a military manner, but in this way the
circle of violence and revenge is continued. Islam remains a sacrificial religion.[1] With respect to the non-monotheistic world religions,
the question should be raised whether awareness of the mechanisms of mimesis and violence can really be said to be restricted
to the Abrahamitic traditions. In this regard, for instance, Leo
Lefebure has defended that awareness of these mechanisms can
also be found in Buddhism and that it is therefore wrong to reject
it as one more sacrificial system.[2] It should of course be noted that
the problem of the relation between Christianity and the other
world religions is not typical for the philosophical Christologies
discussed in this book. Christian theology in general is confronted
with this problem and it may not come as a surprise then that the
so-called 'theology of the religions' is a topic that is high on the
theological agenda. But, it is a matter which becomes especially
urgent when we begin to reflect on the question of the uniqueness of Christianity, a question which is, as we have pointed out at
the end of Chapter 1, unavoidable in the current situation. When
searching for answers on this question, it is very tempting to
reduce the other religions, in a Hegelian way, to precursors which
find their fulfilment in Christianity, which is then designated as

---

[1] René Girard, 'Ce qui se joue aujourd'hui est une rivalité mimétique à l'échelle
planétaire' [interview], *Le Monde*, 6 November 2001. An English translation of
this interview is available on-line: http://www.uibk.ac.at/theol/cover/girard_
le_monde_interview.html (access on December 27, 2007).

[2] Leo D. Lefebure, 'Mimesis, Violence, and Socially Engaged Buddhism:
Overture to a Dialogue', *Contagion* 3 (1996), pp. 121–140. This article can be
read online at: http://www.uibk.ac.at/theol/cover/contagion/contagion03_
Lefebure.pdf (access on 27 December, 2007).

the 'highest' or 'final' religion. The major challenge for the future precisely consists in developing answers to the uniqueness of Christianity which do not fall in this trap of Hegelianism.

Of the answers to the question of the uniqueness of Christianity presented in the current volume, the one of Girard seems to be the most promising. Not only does it receive convergent support from recent developments within the natural sciences and does it enable us to accept modernity *critically*, it is also the only philosophical Christology of the ones discussed here that brings us to the threshold of faith. In contrast to Vattimo and Žižek, who abolish all transcendence, Girard points us towards a transcendence of Love that surpasses our human abilities and from which human beings may expect something. For Vattimo and Žižek, in contrast, Christianity is the religion of love precisely because nothing is left behind. Everything is given. Or, to use the words of Caputo, all the divine goods have been transferred to humankind[3] and nothing is to be expected for the future. In this situation there is simply no longer room for *faith*, but only for *knowledge* about how the transfer took place. Offering an account of this transfer is precisely what Vattimo and Žižek are doing in their Christologies. Also in this respect they turn out to be faithful heirs of Hegel. Was it not Hegel who stated that the pictorial thinking of Christianity should be sublated into the true thinking of philosophy?

This is not to deny, however, that even for a Girardian Christology the work has only just begun. As we have indicated in the course of our study, Girard's Christology is in need of being developed further: (1) its Biblical foundation needs to be worked out in more detail, (2) Girard's interpretation of Nietzsche is in need of further elaboration, just like (3) his view on the development of modernity (as presented by Vanheeswijck) and, finally, (4) we have to take Girard into inter-religious dialogue.

---

[3] Caputo and Vattimo, *After the Death of God*, p. 80.

# Bibliography

Altizer, Thomas J. J., *The Gospel of Christian Atheism* (Philadelphia, PA: The Westminster Press, 1966).

Blackmore, Susan, *The Meme Machine* (Oxford: Oxford University Press, 2000).

Boersma, Hans, *Violence, Hospitality, and the Cross: Reappropriating the Atonement Tradition* (Grand Rapids, MI: Baker Academic, pb. edn, 2006).

Boeve, Lieven, *Interrupting Tradition: An Essay on Christian Faith in a Postmodern Context* (trans. Brian Doyle; Louvain Theological and Pastoral Monographs, 30; Leuven and Dudley, Massachusetts, MA: Peeters Press and W. B. Eerdmans, 2003).

—*God Interrupts History: Theology in Times of Upheaval* (London and New York, NY: Continuum, 2007).

Butler, Judith, Ernesto Laclau, and Slavoj Žižek, *Contingency, Hegemony, Universality: Contemporary Dialogues on the Left* (Phronesis; London and New York, NY: Verso, 2000).

Caputo, John D., and Gianni Vattimo, *After the Death of God* (ed. Jeffrey W. Robins; Insurrections: Critical Studies in Religion, Politics, and Culture; New York, NY: Columbia University Press, 2007).

*Cyprano's Journal Online/Revenge of Global Finance By Slavoj Žižek*, http://www.bestcyrano.org/slavojZizekRevengeofFinance207.htm (access on April 30, 2007).

Dawkins, Richard, *The Selfish Gene* (Oxford and New York, NY: Oxford University Press, new edn, 1989).

—'Viruses of the Mind', *A Devil's Chaplain: Selected Writings* (London: Weidenfeld & Nicolson, 2003) pp. 128–45.

De Kesel, Marc, *Eros & ethiek· Een lectuur van Jacques Lacans Séminaire* VII (Psychoanalyse in tijden van wetenschap, 1; Leuven and Leusden: Acco, 2002).

Dennet, Daniel C., *Darwin's Dangerous Idea: Evolution and the Meanings of Life* (London: The Penguin Press, 1995).

de Wit, Theo W. A., 'The Return to Religion: Vattimo's Reconciliation of Christian Faith and Post-Modern Philosophy', *Bijdragen* 61/4 (2000), pp. 390–411.

Dews, Peter, 'Hegel in Analysis: Slavoj Žižek's Lacanian Dialectics', *Bulletin of the Hegel Society of Great Britain* no. 21/22 (1990), pp. 1–18.

—'The Tremor of Reflection: Slavoj Žižek's Lacanian Dialectics', *Radical Philosophy* no. 72 (1995), pp. 17–29.

Dews, Peter, and Peter Osborne, 'Lacan in Slovenia: An Interview with Slavoj Žižek and Renata Salecl', *Radical Philosophy* no. 58 (1991), pp. 25–31.

# Bibliography

Evans, Dylan, *An Introductory Dictionary of Lacanian Psychoanalysis* (repr., London and New York, NY: Routledge, 1997).

Gallese, Vittorio, Luciano Fadiga, Leonardo Fogassi, Giacomo Rizzolatti, 'Action Recognition in the Premotor Cortex', *Brain* 119 (1996), pp. 593–609.

Garrels, Scott R., 'Imitation, Mirror Neurons & Mimetic Desire: Convergent Support for the Work of René Girard' [paper presented during the 2004 annual conference of the Colloquium on Violence and Religion (COV&R)]. The paper can be read on line at: http://girardianlectionary.net/covr2004/garrelspaper.pdf (access on December 10, 2007).

Girard, René, *Mensonge romantique et vérité romanesque* (Paris: Editions Bernard Grasset, 1961).

—*Deceit, Desire, and the Novel: Self and Other in Literary Structure* (trans. Yvonne Treccero; Baltimore, MD and London: The Johns Hopkins Press, 1965).

—*La Violence et le sacré* (Paris: Editions Bernard Grasset, 1972).

—*Des choses cachées depuis la fondation du monde* (Paris: Editions Grasset & Fasquelle, 1978).

—'Dionysus versus the Crucified', *MLN* 99/4 (1984), pp. 816–35.

—*Things Hidden Since the Foundation of the World* (research undertaken in collaboration with Jean-Michel Oughourlian and Guy Lefort; trans. Stephen Bann and Michael Metteer; London: The Athlone Press, 1987).

—'The Founding Murder in the Philosophy of Nietzsche', *Violence and Truth: On the Work of René Girard* (ed. Paul Dumouchel; London: The Athlone Press, 1988) pp. 227–46.

—*Violence and the Sacred* (trans. Patrick Gregory; London: The Athlone Press, 1995).

—'Dionysus versus the Crucified', *The Girard Reader* (ed. James G. Williams; repr., New York, NY: Crossroad Publishing, 2003) pp. 243–61.

—'Ce qui se joue aujourd'hui est une rivalité mimétique à l'échelle planétaire' [interview], *Le Monde*, November 6, 2001. An English translation of this interview is available on line: http://www.uibk.ac.at/theol/cover/girard_le_monde_interview.html (access on December 27, 2007).

—*Les origines de la culture: Entretiens avec Pierpaolo Antonello et Joao Cezar de Castro Rocha* (Paris: Desclée de Brouwer, 2004).

—*Evolution and Conversion: Dialogues on the Origins of Culture* (with Joao Cezar de Castro Rocha and Pierpaolo Antonello; London and New York, NY: T&T Clark, 2008).

Glynos, Jason, 'Symptoms of a Decline in Symbolic Faith, or, Žižek's Anti-capitalism', *Paragraph* 24/2 (2001), pp. 78–110.

Heiser, Marc, Marco Iacoboni, Fumiko Maeda, Jake Marcus, John C. Mazziotta, 'The Essential Role of Broca's Area in Imitation', *European Journal of Neuroscience* 17/5 (2003), pp. 1123–28.

Homer, Sean, 'It's the Political Economy, Stupid! On Žižek's Marxism', *Radical Philosophy* no. 108 (2001), pp. 7–16.

Iacoboni, Marco, 'Neural Mechanisms of Imitation', *Current Opinion in Neurobiology* 15 (2005), pp. 632–37.

# Bibliography

Iacoboni, Marco, Roger P. Woods, Marcel Brass, Harold Bekkering, John C. Mazziotta, Giacomo Rizzolatti, 'Cortical Mechanisms of Human Imitation', *Science* 286/5449 (1999), pp. 2526–28.

Jonkers, Peter, 'In the World, but not of the World: The Prospects of Christianity in the Modern World', *Bijdragen* 61/4 (2000), pp. 370–89.

Kay, Sarah, *Žižek: A Critical Introduction* (Key Contemporary Thinkers; Cambridge: Polity, 2003).

Kerr, Fergus, 'Rescuing Girard's Argument?', *Modern Theology* 8/4 (1992), pp. 385–99.

Leakey, Richard, *The Origin of Mankind* (Science Master series; New York, NY: Basic Books, 1996).

Lefebure, Leo D., 'Mimesis, Violence, and Socially Engaged Buddhism: Overture to a Dialogue', *Contagion* 3 (1996), pp. 121–140. This article can be read on line at: http://www.uibk.ac.at/theol/cover/contagion/contagion03_Lefebure.pdf (access on December 27, 2007).

Lewin, Roger, and Robert A. Foley, *Principles of Human Evolution* (Oxford: Blackwell, 2nd edn, 2004).

Meganck, Erik, *Nihilistische caritas? Secularisatie bij Gianni Vattimo* (Tertium Datur, 15; Leuven: Uitgeverij Peeters, 2005).

Meltzoff, Andrew N., and M. Keith Moore, 'Imitation of Facial and Manual Gestures by Human Neonates', *Science* 198/4312 (1977), pp. 74–78.

Milbank, John, *Theology and Social Theory: Beyond Secular Reason* (Signposts in Theology; repr., Oxford: Blackwell, 1994).

Moriarty, Michael, 'Žižek, Religion and Ideology', *Paragraph* 24/2 (2001), pp. 125–39.

Müller-Lauter, W., 'Nietzsche und Heidegger als nihilistische Denker: Zu Gianni Vattimos "postmodernistischer" Deutung', *Nietzsche-Studien* 27 (1998), pp. 52–81.

Nietzsche, Friedrich, *Werke: Kritische Studienausgabe* (ed. Giorgio Colli and Mazzino Montinari; Berlin and New York, NY: Walter de Gruyter, 1967–).

—*On the Genealogy of Morals/Ecce Homo* (trans. Walter Kaufmann and R. J. Hollingdale; New York, NY: Vintage Books, 1989).

—*Beyond Good and Evil: Prelude to a Philosophy of the Future* (trans. R.J. Hollingdale; intr. Michael Tanner; Penguin Classics; repr. with rev. and new introd., London: Penguin Books, 1990).

—*Writings from the Late Notebooks* (ed. Rüdiger Bittner; trans. Kate Sturge; Cambridge Texts in the History of Philosophy; Cambridge: Cambridge University Press, 2003).

—*The Anti-Christ, Ecce Homo, Twilight of the Idols and Other Writings* (ed. Aaron Ridley and Judith Norman; trans. Judith Norman; Cambridge Texts in the History of Philosophy; Cambridge: Cambridge University Press, 2005).

Populier, Jan, *God heeft echt bestaan: Met René Girard naar een nieuw mens – en wereldbeeld* (Tielt [W.-Vl.]: Lannoo – Mimesis, 1994).

Ramachandran, Vilayanur S., 'Mirror Neurons and Imitation Learning as the Driving Force Behind the "Great Leap Forward" in Human

# Bibliography

Evolution', http://www.edge.org/documents/archive/edge69.html (access on December 10, 2007).

Rizzolatti, Giacomo, and Michael A. Arbib, 'Language within our Grasp', *Trends in Neuroscience* 21/5 (1998), pp. 188–94.

Rizzolatti, Giacomo, and Laila Craighero, 'The Mirror-Neuron System', *Annual Review of Neuroscience* 27 (2004), pp. 169–92.

Rizzolatti, Giacomo, Leonardo Fogassi, Vittorio Gallese, 'Neurophysiological Mechanisms Underlying the Understanding and Imitation of Action', *Nature Reviews: Neuroscience* 2/9 (2001), pp. 661–70.

Schillebeeckx, Edward, 'Secularization and Christian Belief in God', *God the Future of Man* (trans. N. D. Smith; Theological Soundings, 5,1; London and Sydney: Sheed and Ward, 1969) pp. 51–90.

Sciglitano, Anthony C., jr., 'Contesting the World and the Divine: Balthasar's Tritinitarian "Response" to Gianni Vattimo's Secular Christianity', *Modern Theology* 23/4 (2007), pp. 525–59.

Taylor, Matthew, 'From Memetics to Mimetics: Richard Dawkins, René Girard, and Media-Related Pathologies' [paper presented during the 2002 annual conference of the Colloquium on Violence and Religion (COV&R)], p. 3. Unfortunately, this paper is no longer available online.

Valadier, Paul, *Nietzsche et la critique du christianisme* (Cogitatio fidei, 77; Paris: Les Editions du Cerf, 1974).

—*Jésus-Christ ou Dionysos: La foi chrétienne en confrontation avec Nietzsche* (Jésus et Jésus-Christ, 10; Paris: Desclée, 1979).

Van Haute, Philippe, *Against Adaptation: Lacan's Subversion of the Subject* (trans. Paul Crowe *et al.*; The Lacanian Clinical Field; New York, NY: Other Press, 2002).

Vanheeswijck, Guido, *Voorbij het onbehagen: Ressentiment en christendom* (Leuven: Davidsfonds, 2002).

van Knippenberg, Tjeu, 'Transcendence and Personal History/Life Stories', *The Human Image of God* (Festschrift Johannes A. van der Ven; ed. Hans-Georg Ziebert *et al.*; Leiden, Boston, MA, and Köln: Brill, 2001) pp. 263–84.

van Leeuwen, Arend Theodoor, *Christianity in World History: The Meeting of the Faiths of East and West* (trans. Hubert H. Hoskins; forew. Hendrik Kraelmer; London: Edingburgh House Press, 1964).

Vattimo, Gianni, *La avventure della differenza: Che chosa significa pensare dopo Nietzsche e Heidegger* (Milan: Garzanti Editore, 1980).

—'Dialects, Difference, and Weak Thought', *Graduate Faculty Philosophy Journal* 10/1 (1984), pp. 151–64.

—*La fine della modernità: Nichilismo ed ermeneutica nella cultura post-moderna* (Milan: Garzanti Editore, 1985).

—(ed.), *Filosofia '86* (Rome: Gius, Laterza & Figli, 1986).

—*The End of Modernity: Nihilism and Hermeneutics in Post-modern Culture* (trans. and intr. Jon R. Snyder; Cambridge: Polity Press, 1988).

—(ed.), *La sécularisation de la pensée* (trans. Charles Alunni *et al.*; L'ordre philosophique; Paris: Editions du Seuil, 1988).

# Bibliography

—'Metaphysics, Violence, Secularization', *Recoding Metaphysics: The New Italian Philosophy* (ed. Giovanna Borradori; Evanston, IL: Northwestern University Press, 1988) pp. 45–61.

—'Toward an Ontology of Decline', *Recoding Metaphysics: The New Italian Philosophy* (ed. Giovanna Borradori; Evanston, IL: Northwestern University Press, 1988) pp. 63–75.

—*The Adventure of Difference: Philosophy after Nietzsche and Heidegger* (trans. C. Blamires and T. Harrison; Cambridge: Polity Press, 1993).

—*Oltre l'interpretazione: Il significato dell'ermeneutica per la filosofia* (Lezioni Italiane; Rome and Bari: Laterza and Figli, 1994).

—*Credere di credere: È possibile essere cristiani nonostante la Chiesa?* (Milan: Garzanti Editore, 1996).

—*Beyond Interpretation: The Meaning of Hermeneutics for Philosophy* (trans. David Webb; Cambridge: Polity Press, 1997).

—'The Trace of the Trace', *Religion* (ed. Jacques Derrida, Gianni Vattimo, and Hans-Georg Gadamer; Cambridge: Polity Press, 1998) pp. 79–94.

—*Belief* (trans. Luca D'Isanto and David Webb; Cambridge: Polity Press, 1999).

—*Dopo la cristianità: Per un christianesimo non religioso* (Milan: Garzanti Editore, 2002).

—*After Christianity* (Italian Academy Lectures; New York, NY: Columbia University Press, 2002).

Vattimo, Gianni, and Pier Aldo Rovatti (eds), *Il pensiero debole* (Milan: Feltrinelli, 1983).

Woods, Alan, and Ted Grant, *Reason in Revolt: Marxist Philosophy and Modern Science* (Marxism in the New Millennium, 1; London: Wellred Publications, 1995).

Zabala, Santiago (ed.), *Il futuro della Religione: Solidarietà, carità, ironia* (Turin: Garzanti Libri, 2004).

—*The Future of Religion: Richard Rorty and Gianni Vattimo* (New York, NY: Columbia University Press, 2005).

—'Introduction: Gianni Vattimo and Weak Philosophy', *Weakening Philosophy: Essays in Honour of Gianni Vattimo* (ed. Santiago Zabala; Montreal & Kingston, London, and Ithaca: McGill-Queen's University Press, 2007) pp. 3–34.

Žižek, Slavoj *Le plus sublime des hystériques: Hegel passe* (Paris: Point Hors Ligne, 1988).

—*The Sublime Object of Ideology* (Phronesis; London and New York, NY: Verso, 1989).

—*The Plague of Fantasies* (Wo es war; London and New York, NY: Verso, 1997).

—*The Ticklish Subject: The Absent Centre of Political Ontology* (Wo es war; London and New York, NY: Verso, 1999).

—'Preface: Burning the Bridges', *The Žižek Reader* (ed. Edmond and Elizabeth Wright; Blackwell Readers; Oxford: Blackwell, 1999) pp. vii–x.

—*The Fragile Absolute: Or, Why is the Christian Legacy Worth Fighting For?* (Wo es war; London and New York, NY: Verso, 2000).

# Bibliography

—*Did Somebody Say Totalitarianism? Five Interventions in the (Mis)Use of a Notion* (Wo es war; London and New York, NY: Verso, 2001).

—*On Belief* (Thinking in Action; London and New York, NY: Routledge, 2001).

—*The Puppet and the Dwarf: The Perverse Core of Christianity* (Short Circuits; Cambridge, MA: MIT Press, 2003).

—*The Parallax View* (Short Circuits; Cambridge, MA: MIT Press, 2006).

# Index

# Index

# Index